The Impossible Community

Barbara Benjamin

*A Story of
Hardship & Hope
at Brooklyn College
in New York*

*InterVarsity Press
Downers Grove
Illinois 60515*

© 1978 by Inter-Varsity Christian Fellowship
of the United States of America

All rights reserved. No part of this book may
be reproduced in any form without
written permission from InterVarsity Press.

InterVarsity Press is the book-publishing
division of Inter-Varsity Christian Fellowship,
a student movement active on campus
at hundreds of universities, colleges
and schools of nursing. For information about
local and regional activities, write IVCF,
233 Langdon St., Madison, WI 53703.

Distributed in Canada through InterVarsity Press,
1875 Leslie Street, Unit 10, Don Mills,
Ontario M3B 2M5, Canada.

ISBN 0-87784-653-7
Library of Congress Catalog
Card Number: 77-27741

Printed in the United States of America

To the students of Brooklyn
College for making
this story possible

To Marcia, Martha, Marcie,
Judith and Jason
for sharing Thom with us
these last two years

Foreword

The story told in the following pages requires a little preparation. Proper preparation should include an introduction to the author, Barbara Benjamin. But meeting Barbara herself requires some warning, some word of caution.

I was given no such "word" when a fellow undergraduate, Marlene Chisholm, introduced me to her one day at the main gate of the Brooklyn College campus. After our names had been exchanged, Miss Benjamin asked me to attend the next Inter-Varsity meeting. I don't recall whether I mumbled that I was not on any school team, whether I said I did not know what she was talking about, or whether I simply smiled politely, but she explained that Inter-Varsity Christian Fellowship was a fellowship of Christians on campus who met for prayer and Bible study. The invitation was kind enough, but I grew suspicious as the look on this woman's face clearly stated that although she had just met me, she could see where I would fit beautifully into God's plans for Brooklyn College as she saw them.

And "Miss B." is just such a person: intelligent, highly emotional, outspoken, methodical and calculating—for the glory of God. As a believer who deeply knows and trusts the living God, she saw Brooklyn College with its more than thirty thousand, multicultural, multiracial students as the place where the Lord could show his glory through those willing to be the conduits. I had been a Christian for many years before I met Barbara, but rarely had I seen such single-minded devotion to the spreading of his name and such a willingness to take what she calls "*calculated* risk."

Consider yourself a little familiar with Barbara Benjamin. Perhaps now you can guess what kind of story, or rather adventure, is in your hands. The college campus is not always the seat of dispassionate rational inquiry. It can be the eye of a storm, the generator of violence, the place where people and not just ideas are pitted against each other, where bitterness, prejudice, jealousy and hatred can fester and run. It can also be the place where people try to understand fresh ideas, different perspectives, new people.

The Impossible Community is a recollection of what the late sixties and early seventies were like at a secular college when the author helped re-vitalize an almost defunct Inter-Varsity chapter and make it a witness to the complete lordship of Christ. What was "impossible" about this was the community of believers who finally came together: collegians of Oriental, Irish, Hispanic, Norwegian, Black American, Italian, Jewish, Turkish, German and Caribbean descent; Christians whose styles of worship differed sometimes as much as their ethnic backgrounds.

But the Spirit of God made us a united witness.

What we went through, frequently at Miss B.'s instigation, fills these pages. As you read, may you be tempted to take some *"calculated risk"* for the glory of God.

Russell Weatherspoon
The Stony Brook School
Stony Brook, N.Y.

1

New Beginnings

It had happened at last! After nine months of re-orienting my life to these United States, I had gotten the longed-for college teaching position. Indeed I had prayed for some time, especially during November and December when I thought I couldn't take another day at that typewriter in the Columbia University Admissions Office. The job had seemed so appealing when I first started in September because of promised contact with foreign students. But that contact turned out to be minimal. Instead there were hours and hours of typing of forms and letters. My previous ministry in Ecuador had been with people not with machines and paper. As a teacher and a missionary my life had been so varied and fulfilling that now I simply rebelled.

Then suddenly, in the middle of January 1969, the call had come—while at work too! Dean Helen Brell from Brooklyn College of the City University was looking for an instructor of international education and wondered if I might qualify as the Latin American specialist. "Would you mind repeating that?" I almost asked. Here at last was a chance to go back to teaching—and on a secular campus, something I had desired so much.

The next day I was interviewed. As deputy chairman of graduate studies in the School of Education, Dean Brell recommended to the chairman of the school, Dean Rosenzweig, that I be given a full-time position. I was on! I learned later that one of the professors in the department had recommended me. We both had been members of Inter-Varsity Christian Fellowship at Queens College during our undergraduate years. Since it was January, I had been quickly interviewed and then given the assignment.

So my heart's desire was granted, and I thanked God for the series of events that had made it possible. I am glad now that I did not know all that this new venture was to entail. I had been doing some interesting in-depth study of Paul's Epistles to the Thessalonians and Timothy. The words *soldier* and *suffering* stand out in my diaries during that time. I had no idea that this was designed to prepare me for the second stage of my life's ministry.

Paul talked about being proud of the Thessalonians because they were steadfast, enduring and patient in the midst of all their persecutions, crushing distress and afflictions. How could this ever apply to me, a returned missionary, back in the United States?

I will never forget my first impressions of Brooklyn College. How different from Latin America where I had spent the previous eleven years! And yet not completely so: I was again in the minority. This time, however, the majority consisted of about 24,000 Jewish students, 3,000 Italian students and 4,000 "minority" students who were largely Chinese, Blacks or Hispanics. The rest had varied backgrounds. Like me, they were a little of everything.

Now logic, it seemed, would have indicated that of all the branches of the City University, this was a poor choice for me. Surely there were more evangelical or evangelically prone people on any of the other campuses. There were also more Hispanics elsewhere, and I was proficient in the Spanish language and well acquainted with Latin American culture. Yet here I was, thrust into a most hostile and unknown world—as I was soon to learn.

Something about this whole situation, though, presented the kind of challenge I had always wanted: virgin territory without active Christian witness but with an opportunity to prove God in the midst of it all. I had no idea where to find any other Christians or how to begin a Christian witness. I would start completely fresh.

During my first days I had little time to consider such matters. I was engrossed in preparing for classes. Because I was in the School of Education, I not only had to become acquainted with the college setting itself, but I also had to investigate the public schools to find out what I was preparing students for.

I prayed of course and then intuitively set about my business. I told my curriculum classes honestly that I came to them only with book theory and experience in New York City schools that dated from years past. So I planned immediately to visit the present school systems.

Among my students I found a very bright, radical young man, Bob Cohen. I cannot recall if Bob asked me or if I asked Bob, but soon we paired up for visits to a number of public schools. This of course meant a lot of informal conversation and coffee breaks. Bob soon discovered that his instructor had been a teacher in a Protestant seminary in South America and that she was very "religious." I learned from Bob that the word *missionary* is taboo among Jews. So later I avoided using it among my Jewish friends.

Bob was a great help to me in other ways. He introduced me to all the relevant radical writers of the time, like Marcuse and Roszak. Through Bob I also became friends with Meyer Kantor, the faculty sponsor of the Young Socialists at Brooklyn

College, a Jew who admired Jesus as the ideal revolutionary.

Bob's orientation to campus life and thinking were important for another reason. It was the spring semester of 1969. By April the atmosphere on campus was so tense, particularly over Vietnam and other local issues, that the police were brought in to assure continued academic pursuits. I well remember the strikes both in 1969 and 1970. I walked around the campus listening to the rhetoric, sensing the pervading mood.

I recall actually hating Bart Meyers, an able professor in the psychology department, who was also a gifted engineer of mob psychology. He could move these unknowledgeable and unthinking young students at his whim—or so it seemed. Thanks to him and others like him the White SDS (Students for a Democratic Society) mocked and spat upon the police who were assigned to the campus. I can remember especially the emotions I felt against him and the leftists when twenty Blacks and Puerto Ricans were picked up by the police in the middle of the night for disturbing the peace on campus!

As I watched all of this, and prayed, I wondered what God would do and what in the world I was to do. I was picking up all the literature pouring into the campus from various sources. I found that most of it had the same message I had seen in Latin America except that now the objects of attack were more local. Was this simply leftist propaganda or was something seriously wrong in our society?

It was early May 1969, and except for one very kind and friendly liberal Protestant colleague, I still had not sighted a Christian or seen any sign of one! There were no posters on the billboards and no Christian literature to be seen. I had asked for prayer about all this at Hephzibah House, a Christian residence where I lived temporarily. Here a nucleus of mature Christians were praying daily for local problems, national issues and world missions. It seemed as if I wasn't doing anything in the midst of this turmoil. I didn't realize that God was giving me time to get my bearings in this new world.

God showed me that he lives, that he has a perfect timing for everything and that he knows what he is doing. Bob one day turned to a Chinese student in my class and told her that the instructor of the course was religious and even had been a missionary. Lois could hardly believe him. After all, most of the instructors at Brooklyn College had a Jewish background and my last name was Benjamin. There was only one way to find out. So Miss Wong gathered up her courage and approached me.

She told me that Bob had talked to her about my experiences in Latin America and inquired in good, indirect Oriental style about why I had gone abroad. As I began to explain how God had called me to serve him—and I had a terrible time getting this into more vernacular terms—she smiled and told me that she too was a Christian. What is more, she told me how she and a few other "Bible" Christian students had decided to have Bible study and prayer on a regular basis. She explained that they were looking for a faculty sponsor. Would I be interested in telling the little group about my experiences in Latin America?

I was excited. Within a few days I found myself at SUBO, the Student Building, sitting with six Christian students: two Irish-Italians, two Chinese and two Blacks. They said that there were other Christians around but that it was difficult to get them together. I also discovered that Inter-Varsity Christian Fellowship was a chartered club on campus but that in recent years it had not been active. It was May and finals would begin in a few weeks. It seemed best to find out how to renew the charter and tentatively think about plans for the new school year. I gladly accepted sponsorship of the group.

The summer came. I spent some time at a Bible Conference in Massachusetts. I asked God to reassure me about teaching at Brooklyn College. Then a missionary speaker from New York flashed a slide of Brooklyn College on the screen. I was thrilled. Surely it was his will that I continue there.

2

The Impossible Community

Suddenly it was fall. At my request I was to teach a general course in education along with the graduate course on education in world dimensions. The former dealt with current sociological, cultural, historical and philosophical issues in education. It was closer to my new interest and my knowledge than the curriculum course I had been assigned previously. Both required more study on my part and gave me natural reasons for involvement with the Christian students. They helped me relate my Latin American experiences realistically to contemporary education in the United States.

I was meeting with Artie and Mary Ann Goyena,

Arnold Ng, Bob Sanders and Marlene Chisholm, the nucleus of the reactivated IVCF chapter. We simply planned out two meetings a week. One was a Bible study (we discussed the book of Matthew all year), and the other was a topically oriented forum which enabled us to develop a Christian perspective on current issues on campus: war, sex, the new morality, race, abortion, behavioral psychology, evolution and so on. We also scheduled prayer meetings according to the hours at least a few of us had free at the same time. This was a hassle each semester. We could measure our success both by the careful scheduling we did or did not do and by how much we actually prayed.

Artie Goyena, an Irish-Italian, was president our first year, 1969-70. He was a math major and a good organizer. He was low-keyed, the perfect leader for what I call our year of consolidation. Nothing dramatic happened. In fact, we failed miserably—literally fell apart—at the crisis hour in the spring of 1970.

Some things were accomplished, however, and these became a part of the tradition of the chapter. Developing these unchangeables gave structure and stability to our chapter but left room for individuality and flexibility. The structure was especially important when everything around us was in ferment.

To our basic weekly meetings and small group prayer meetings we added another key ingredient. We decided to copy other groups on the campus and adopt booktable evangelism. We selected the most appropriate literature: tracts, pamphlets and books. We placed our table inside Whitehead Hall, the most highly trafficked area on campus. There we were alongside the Young Socialists, the Students for a Democratic Society, the Abortion Association and the Black Club. Later the Puerto Rican Alliance, the Gay Liberation Front and the Jewish Defense League (JDL) joined the scene as the Young Socialists waned and the SDS disappeared.

At first we were scared. Sometimes during a break or lunch hour I just hung around the table for moral support. Once we really got going, the students were anxious to continue this outreach. Through this table we were able to "find" other Christians as well as to exchange views with others. When the table was not put up, I would try to find out why. Usually the problem was either a lost key to my office, where materials were kept, or some other organizational breakdown. These were discussed and prayed about, and students began taking their responsibilities for this ministry more seriously.

The table was a natural for the college atmosphere. It was also a place where inexperienced Christians could find support until they learned how better to answer questions about their faith and until they were convinced themselves that Scripture really was relevant on a twentieth-century, humanistic-secular university campus. The table was also a place for fellowship and mutual encouragement. Singing the latest contemporary Christian songs at the table was often a real drawing card. After all, who in the world sang in those depressing days, especially joyful songs of hope! We would sing about a spark that could be passed on, "Walking with Jesus," "The Man of Galilee," and Somebody who was everything to us! Even if the noise was not always appreciated by adjoining tables, it always drew people for questions and discussion.

And some of those songs were extra special! The members of the fellowship could sing with such melody and rhythm and harmony! I wish you could have heard Frank Colon and Danny Velasquez sing their own creation:

Do you know my Jesus? Do you know my Lord?
Do you know he's faithful, walking down that
road?
People watching as he passes by
They don't know that my Lord is passing by!
Oh! There's something you must know—
That no matter how wrong you've been
My Jesus loves you so!

They would sing that song; then we would join in. I felt as if my heart would burst with yearning for the passers-by to know that Jesus really did love them! Rose Lee was another of our famous musicians. She would string that guitar, and we were on the way to a marvelous public expression of our joy and faith and hope in Jesus Christ. Russ Weatherspoon, Bryan Best and Cheryl Chisholm were among our inspiring song leaders too.

One of our biggest difficulties was to develop a sense of community. This is a natural problem on a commuter campus. It was much easier when I was a student at Queens College. Most of us were White, came from more or less the same evangelical churches and the same socioeconomic class. Now, however, we had students from different ethnic groups and different socioeconomic classes in the club. We also had many more international students. Thanks to the leftist rhetoric, our consciousness about interracial relationships had been aroused. We determined to do what they talked about but were never able to realize. We worked very idealistically on cross-cultural relations. In Christ this is possible, though not as easy as we had anticipated.

Our White population was also mixed. It included a very few third-generation evangelical students. Most of their families had fled the city. We also had a number of charismatic Catholics. There were some who had become Christian disciples through our own efforts, like Thelma DeVine, Ginnie Sullo, Mike Benvengo, Arnold Greenwald and Robin Kostletter. They were either Catholic or Jewish in background. There were also some White Europeans who came through the fellowship, like Elias, our Greek friend, who found Bible study and spontaneous prayer so refreshing in contrast to his more liturgical church. Harold Daasvand, whose father edited the only Norwegian paper in

New York City, was given a solid grounding in the Word while with us. He later wrote from Norway that IVCF had helped him enormously in surviving the rationalistic theology of the Lutheran State Seminary he attends. We also had a Turkish girl, Haver, who attended regularly, though she never did give up her Moslem religion as far as we know.

Our society often considers Blacks to be a homogeneous group, but they are really quite heterogeneous. There are the Caribbean Blacks. Most of these have come from the formerly British colonies and speak formal English with a bit of a British accent. Many have had the advantage of a strong educational background. Several in this group have been members of our chapter, including Tony Warner (now on IVCF staff), all four of the Barnetts (Gideon, Curtis, Morley and Reina) and Bryan Best (who went on to finish graduate work in biochemistry at New Orleans University).

In New York there are also some three hundred thousand Creole-speaking, French-reading Haitians who are refugees from that poverty stricken island. We have always had a few of them in the club. One Haitian student looked for refuge in IVCF and diligently sought consolation in Christ while suffering from severe culture shock. He eventually had to leave school because of a series of problems. We had at least shown him the way to Christ and tried to understand him and relate to his needs.

There were also Blacks who come from (formerly British) Guyana on the northern coast of South America. George Cummings, whose father is still a medical doctor in Guyana, accepted Christ through Russ Weatherspoon's witness while still in high school. He grew in Christ through IVCF. He later transferred to Gordon College to complete his studies. Now he is in seminary, preparing for Christian service.

Blacks from Africa, whom we easily dump into one group but who are very different in physiognomy, custom and beliefs, make up another group. In the New York area the Nigerians predominate, and we have two or three lifelong friendships. Some had been influenced by Christian missions in their countries. One of them, Sam, had an Anglian background in Nigeria, and grew in love and in the Word through the club. He finished all of his studies in geology at Brooklyn College in three years. Then, through a graduate assistantship, he completed his master's too. Desi Osuagu also joined us after having been very confused by the dominant American culture. Eventually he received Christ as his Savior and attended the church of one of our members while he was in Brooklyn.

The most difficult group to evangelize at Brooklyn College was and still is the Black American. This group has been very separatist: Blacks have been hostile to any within their group who have joined our chapter. This is more because we are an integrated group than because we are Christian, though the latter too was an anathema during the years of the renaissance of the Black Muslims. Certainly as I watched "Roots" I could understand more fully the interrelationship of both factors, the White culture and the White religion. Students had to make the difficult choice between being Christian first and then Black or being Black and then Christian.

We discovered as we fellowshiped together that often there were unconscious hostile attitudes among Blacks and Whites. One second-generation American Black whose grandparents came from Barbados simply could not stand southern Blacks. The Black Americans in our group, on the other hand, tended to resent the less hostile and more determined attitudes of the Caribbean Blacks and to see them as Uncle Toms. Secretly, these Black Americans often admired the inner security of the Caribbean Blacks because they seldom have the scars which result from having had to face the alienating prejudices of the dominant White society all of their lives. The Caribbean Blacks in the chapter often felt that Black Americans were anti-intellectual. Initially, they do not usually have the hopelessness that Black Americans have acquired from an early age nor realize the deficiencies of both southern and northern ghetto schools.

I do not want to give the impression that the Caribbean Blacks are unaware of hostile feelings toward Blacks in our country. Some of my counseling has been with Caribbean Blacks who truly suffered because they could not assume a subservient role which our dominant society silently and forcibly expected of them. Some were able to find peace with God and with themselves through the forgiveness Christ offers through the cross. For others this attitude was not possible. It meant, in their eyes, a loss of their personal dignity and worth. In many ways I can identify with Caribbean Blacks because of my own experience as a "Black." Like them, I have walked into a world which is painful and unexpected. It has demanded that I totally re-evaluate American society and how I am to cope with it.

Another ethnic group which seems closed to outsiders is the Orientals. In New York they are mostly Chinese, more from Cantonese-speaking Hong Kong than from Mandarin-speaking Taiwan —but members of both groups have been in our chapter. Some are second- or third-generation mainland Chinese of an entirely different dialect. The ABC (American-born Chinese) does not seem to be bothered by these differences in background. Chinese can seem passive, but are actually self-disciplined, highly motivated, very studious and well organized. There are exceptions, however, to every rule. While Arnold Ng, Ernie Chin, Faith Low, Wendy Yee, Maynor Moy and Winfred Chin might fit the above description, Dexter Yee is more outgoing and Rose Lee is an intense, verbal and dreamy musician. The Orientals could be easily

lost, however, in the shuffle of Black and Hispanic
exuberance and charisma if one were not careful
and aware.

Of course, I have not yet said a word about the
Hispanics—so attractive in personality, so easily
enthused and so readily distracted! In New York,
Puerto Ricans (PRs, as they call themselves) of the
second generation are beginning to come through
college. There are other Hispanic students, among
them Cubans, who are viewed by most PRs with
feelings of rivalry. Students are coming from all
over Latin America at this time because of economic instability in their own countries and the increasing possibility of bilingual job openings here.
(The United States now has the fifth largest Spanish-speaking population in the world!)

Danny and Frank were our outstanding musical
PRs. They sang us to fame and glory on the quad,
at the booktable and at faculty teas. Eventually
Frank married a Paraguayan girl and had lead roles
in musical presentations produced by the music
department. Rachel Borges, from a strong Christian home, was attracted to our club for a while
and took some new ideas to her Spanish church.
More recently, Naomi Lopez had a significant
leadership role. However, most Hispanics do not
stay long in our group because of strong language
and cultural ties to their communities and
churches. Yet, IVCF offered much to them in leadership training and in acculturation to the dominant society. The former is needed because there

are few trained pastors or lay leaders in Spanish churches. The latter is needed for a successful launch into the American job market.

What a challenge to try to understand all of these groups! What a challenge to the power of the gospel and the work of the Holy Spirit to have all these groups represented in the fellowship and truly accepting and loving one another. It defied all sociological laws—and even "church growth" patterns.

And what could one do with this lovely conglomeration of people to create a genuine feeling of commitment to one another, and a desire to form a community of believers? Intuition told me that our greatest need was for more direct and prolonged contact with each other. How could this be done on a commuter campus? After prayer and thought we began (and each year since 1970 have continued) an inter-session retreat. Inter-session weeks are, agreeably, in January, just after the fall semester exams and before the spring semester. According to how rich or poor we are (or what connections we have) we travel by car or bus up the river to Hudson House, an Inter-Varsity retreat center in Nyack, New York, for at least a weekend. The retreat is organized by a committee selected by the executive committee (the key leaders in the chapter). The staff member and faculty sponsor cooperate.

I find that my biggest role outside of counseling or helping to prepare appropriate Bible study material is being a chaperone. I have to convince Black, Hispanic or Oriental parents that their daughters will be safe and that I will guard them with my life. I go to their homes or talk by phone with parents and reassure them that all will be well. I learned in Ecuador first and then from the students here that young ladies generally do not sleep away from home except with special permission. I also tell frustrated students how fortunate they are to have parents who have standards that show they care for them.

These weekends, I have found, are excellent for leadership development, fun and fellowship, working out any hang-ups within the group, and preparing spiritually for another semester together. Often brothers, sisters and friends from other colleges accompany us to these retreats. This is a normal occurrence among some of these cultural groups and presents a natural opportunity for evangelism and sharing our faith more by action than by words.

In all this, within two years we had built into our annual plans certain permanent ingredients: Bible studies, prayer meetings, topical discussions, table evangelism and the midyear retreat. Through these stable elements we were able to form a community which seemed impossible to some Christians but not to God.

3

Christ, Cambodia and Confrontation

In addition to our regular programs, we learned to accommodate our Christian witness to the immediate environment and circumstances. Our failures helped us see our need. In 1970 we were unprepared for the Kent State upheaval and the ensuing strikes on campus. We were not yet cohesive enough. Neither did we know how to apply Christian principles to the different situations.

I remember running into Russ Weatherspoon right after the news about the Kent students reached us. He, like me, was trying to minister to many students who were strewn all over campus in emotional disarray. We were each attempting feebly to discuss issues and to witness. "What would Christ say to all of this?" I asked. He gave me his silent treatment. He usually did when he did not know what to say, did not want to say what he knew or when he sensed that I was in a rather emotional state of mind. Somehow, though, I knew that we would develop some contingency plans.

And we did! The next year Nixon invaded Cambodia during the very week that we had scheduled an outreach on the quadrangle, having cleared it with the administration beforehand. The quad is a large open space in the middle of the campus. It was frequented by many students during class changes and club hours, especially in good weather. Our chapter felt inhibited by public appearances. In fact, we were scared to death. We felt inadequate and inferior. I chided them rather incessantly about being cowards "just" because they were largely minority students, though I too was afraid. Nevertheless, we were working hard on a skit and music, and Russ was going to "speechify."

The invasion of Cambodia unnerved us even more because the coalition of leftist groups called our officers and told them that it was their moral obligation to postpone whatever programs we had. We were to allow them to have the quad to protest the new thrust in the war. When we did not cave in, they threatened to take over without our permission or that of the administration. I strongly encouraged our officers not to change their plans, and Russ, who was the president, felt that the best strategy was to promise to give them the quad after our program was over but before our scheduled time ended. This seemed reasonable enough to them. So they advertised their activity and we advertised ours.

The result was unexpected. We had rented an excellent amplifying system from a Black gospel group led by Glen, one of the club members. There before us, behind us, to the sides of us sat and stood the major portion of the radical left-wing of the campus as well as many other concerned students and faculty. I was so excited and nervous that everything was irritating and seemed all wrong. The students in the chapter seemed to arrive later than usual and be less organized than ever. But there we were. Some wondered if the whole club should sing—after all, we were just amateurs. I felt that the spontaneous singing would have an impact. It would be obvious that we were singing to express something more than musical virtuosity.

I don't think that the club ever sang better in its entire history. The rhythm and the harmony spilled out in a most creative way. The group had been working on a pantomime. In a number of scenes we presented various social ills of the day: war, race, sex, drugs. We used posters with current names to suggest current inadequate answers: Marcuse, Skinner, Huxley. The skit closed with testimonies, brief and spontaneous, of answers found through faith in Jesus Christ. Danny, Frank, Jack and Russ sang contemporary gospel songs. They were a testimony in themselves—two Puerto

Ricans, one Black and a very blonde White. The audience listened in complete silence.

Then Russ addressed the group. He was low-keyed, almost philosophical in mood, but he used all of the contemporary jargon. With intensity he asked the group if our problem did not stem less from the war than from the demoralization of society. I smiled to myself, for there were strong Schaefferian overtones to his talk. I recalled the intellectual experience we had had only a few weeks before. Russ had taken several chapter meetings to explain, discuss and explore Francis Schaeffer's *Escape from Reason*. Now Russ persisted in his speech at the quad: did we really have the right to point a finger at the hypocrisy and dishonesty of our government leaders when we too as students were cheating, lying and robbing?

He used some indicting words found in the Scriptures without mentioning the source and closed with some remarks about the need of each individual to repent and face his own need. Christ could change our lives. He could change our country. I liked his casual appearance, his old jeans and messy shirt. I liked his low-keyed yet intense tone. I liked the way he contemporized the words of Scripture without weakening their meaning. The students then quietly distributed New Testaments to all who wanted them—and many did.

The leftists made no attempt to rush us nor to interrupt our program. I know that the sympathetic and friendly sponsor of the Young Socialists was partly responsible for this, humanly speaking. I am sure too that they did not want to appear disrespectful to a largely minority group. The total lack of restlessness though, during the time which they had wanted so sorely was, I am sure, the power of truth and the Word of God. The joy that flooded my soul after two previous years of failure in crisis was overwhelming. When the leftists took over, they enacted a scene in which both Agnew and Nixon were killed, but it all seemed hollow. We now had a corner on the debate. With God's help we would hold on tenaciously.

In the following year God gave us another opportunity to give a Christian witness by not running away from a problem on campus. New York, as you know, is atypical in that all groups are minority groups in the context of the whole United States. However, the large Jewish population, which now dominates many professional, political and civil organizations, was increasingly viewed by the other minorities as being part of the establishment. As open admission policies became a reality and more and more Blacks and Puerto Ricans were coming through the educational system and getting into the job market, a kind of paranoia set in. This has been especially true during the years of recession when both Jews and Blacks feared, and not without reason, for their job security.

Thus strong hostilities developed between Blacks and Jews at Brooklyn College. They met in different areas of the campus and different parts of the cafeterias. These hostilities were not lessened when a "Kosher King" cafeteria was opened and nothing comparable was offered to other minority groups. The largely Jewish administration justified this on the basis of the percentages these groups represented on campus, but it was poor public relations. In an argument over the juke box in the basement of the Student Building (SUBO), a riot broke out between Blacks and Jews. Plans were laid by both sides for a full-scale confrontation. Calls for reinforcements were made by the Panthers and by the Jewish Defense League (JDL). The latter were determined that "never again" would they quietly defer to any other group.

That day Inter-Varsity was holding a meeting on the second floor of SUBO where the heavy drug users met. We had, in addition to music, some ex-addicts from Teen Challenge to testify to the power of Christ that changed and freed them. The meeting was not going well, however. The ex-addicts felt threatened by the college setting. Most of them had not finished high school: they were frightened and showed it.

Suddenly our meeting was interrupted. A number of people cleared out of the room quickly. Some Black faculty members warned the Black students to go home. It was extremely dangerous for them on two counts: they were greatly outnumbered, and they were most likely to be picked up by the police.

The IVCF members gathered around and decided that Christ would not run away from this situation. Deep problems requiring long-term solutions had started the trouble. But we felt responsible to provide some immediate response as well. We left the Student Building and some of the students ran up to my office where we had a few signs reading, "Love Your Neighbor As Yourself" and "Love Your Enemies." We also took all of the poster material and markers. As quickly as possible we hung up the posters in strategic places all over campus. We also handed out tracts, particularly the "Love" tract with the simple quotation from 1 Corinthians 13, printed attractively with a psychedelic cover by the American Bible Society. As fast as we got the signs up, they were being ripped down. We did not stop, however, as we could hear the siren of the riot squad sent from the police precinct. The cars and trucks came roaring down just as the JDL jeeps were rushing in with all of their arms, sticks, knives and guns. The Panthers soon followed.

I cannot remember all that happened; I only remember that I wanted the fellowship to sing again so badly, especially the songs "I Looked for Love" and "We Are One in the Spirit." It seemed as if everything was keeping us from pulling together as the Christians, Black and White, painted signs and ran to put them up while others gave out tracts. I remember the shudder that went through us when I actually saw that riot squad fully armed.

Only then did I grasp what was going on. With my knees trembling, I grabbed Marlene and called those around and said, "Let's pray." Blacks and Whites huddled together, held hands firmly, and prayed out loud for peace and love, for restoration of rationality and sanity.

Then I had to go to class! The last thing I felt like doing was teaching, but I firmly believed that unless classes were canceled by the administration I should be on the job. A bit crestfallen because the Christians had not yet sung, I left. When class was over, I met a few of my Jewish students. They had heard the group singing about loving your neighbors.

"Miss Benjamin, tell that group we do not all hate Blacks!" The student was right. I had many Jewish colleagues and students, like Trudy Berger and Bob Cohen, who had no hostile feelings toward Blacks but who consciously encouraged their vocational pursuits. We hoped that these responsible Jews would act to discourage the JDL's outrageous inciting of a minority group.

"I know you don't all feel that way," I said. "The world needs to know it too." I praised God, for again in a highly tense and emotional situation, we had been able to live and sing an answer that preaching could not have communicated.

4

Urbana
in Black
and White

Though we were able to come to grips with racial attitudes through the topical sessions the chapter offered and by confronting the student world as a racially integrated group, still there were many troubled hearts among our Christian students. We all, Black and White, came from homes which had conditioned us. We were all a part of the American culture: it was unrealistic to deny it.

We were forced to face ourselves and God's Word on this issue at Urbana 70, Inter-Varsity's triennial missionary convention. Twelve members of our newly formed chapter got on the buses to head for Champaign/Urbana, Illinois. Our group was placed on the Soul Liberation II bus. Inside were members of the Soul Liberation Black music group and students from all backgrounds. We had a wonderful time both going and coming from the conference, especially as we sang all kinds of "Soul Lib" songs. We all sang so feelingly, so enthusiastically, so harmoniously—and it was so contagious! We already knew some of the songs and the rest came easily.

I never dreamed that when we arrived at Urbana there would be such a conflagration. We were housed with most of the other urban groups so that the special sessions which had been set up with Tom Skinner and Bill Pannell could be attended easily. The Black Americans in our chapter certainly identified with Skinner and Pannell, and while my own "White" emotions were stirred negatively and positively by Skinner's plenary address, I deeply appreciated his sessions for Blacks only.

I should explain here something which still continues to be a wonder to me and which will explain a previous comment about my own "Black" experience. At Brooklyn College I had encouraged every Christian I met to come to the club. I found some Blacks more open to invitations and to spiritual things in general than others. Probably more West Indians took the initiative to visit the club than any other group of Blacks. Few Whites responded, seemingly because the majority of them were Jewish.

One day before Urbana I bumped into a long,

lanky Black fellow on a bicycle. In his basket was a Bible. I invited him to come to the meeting too. His name was Russell Weatherspoon. I did not know that he would be used greatly by God in the next four years in the club. He told me later that he looked me over carefully. He decided that he would take the risk. He started to attend regularly and soon it was clear that while Artie, an Irish-Italian, was our formal leader, Russ was the informal one. He knew and explained well the Word of God, was a marvelous singer and was loaded with charisma and personality. Thelma and Ginnie, two White girls, among others accepted Christ through Russ's message at the freshman reception.

Russ had become aware of my "whiteness" shortly before Urbana. That day, after some discussion, I had admitted with chagrin that the mission board I previously served under was completely White. It was with some hesitation that he finally told me that he had assumed that I was Black. I remembered his questions, " . . . one hundred per cent White, Miss B.—totally and completely?" I had been living in tension and anxiety in those days as a White faculty sponsor. I feared that the Black students might resent my counsel. This anxiety was carried over easily from my missionary days in Ecuador where I had found that my national friends sometimes resented North American intrusion. I am inclined to be direct in sharing my ideas. This is not only the influence of American culture but a trait which all seven of my siblings acquired from our dad.

I should also say to my readers that I am olive-skinned with, as Russ says, many facial features (mouth and cheekbones particularly) which could be seen as one who had Black antecedents. My direct manner was not seen as unusual for a Black woman, so Russ had found it easy to relate to me. I felt immense relief when Russ told me this. (I now knew why Black faculty and students sought me out on campus. Obviously these physical features, somewhat formal dress habits and certain speaking gestures acquired in South America had given me a distinct advantage at an important time in my ministry.)

Other factors accounted for my acceptance by Blacks. They saw me as very empathetic to them and their problems. While it has been a strange experience to be considered Black after having been brought up in a White home in New York City, many experiences gradually heightened my awareness of the Black situation.

Initially, my parents instilled a good deal of racial tolerance in me. Dad's influence was less because he was often away from our home working long hours to support a family of seven children. Mom was the daughter of Polish immigrants. She knew what it was like to be treated as an outsider, and she would not let us be unkind or unfriendly to anyone. My parents even consented when a Puerto Rican asked me to go with him to the junior high-school graduation prom. That was unheard of in our neighborhood.

Mom realized, however, that Bushwick High School, where I should have been assigned, was deteriorating. She reported to the school that my address had been changed to another area where my aunt resided. Thus I could attend a better high school. I did not realize until I returned from Ecuador that the Bushwick area was becoming Black and Puerto Rican and that mom and dad had worried about this. They wanted me to do well in school so I could attend the City University. I ended up at Grover Cleveland High School, on the border between Queens and Brooklyn. It was a predominantly White school with high academic standards. From there I went to Queens College.

There were few Blacks at Queens College in the fifties. One Black Christian attended the Inter-Varsity chapter and we became friends. She invited me to her home. I never went because she lived in a bad neighborhood. I do not remember what happened to her; she just disappeared from our group, it seems. I think we failed her.

After I finished my studies at Queens I spent two years at Nyack College, made up of many students from the Midwest and especially from western Pennsylvania. There may have been one or two Black students there. I studied Bible, missions and anthropology in preparation for Christian service abroad. I also taught at a private Christian high school in Georgia as part of a home service requirement. The students were White with a small number of Cubans. Local Blacks were employed only as porters, maids or farm hands.

The academy often invited outside speakers for chapel. One Black preacher visited us at least twice in the two years I was there. I learned at his first visit that he was not allowed to eat in the dining room because of what the town folk would say. He was entertained in the home of the vice president, but I entered with vehemence into the discussion about the matter. There were a number of northern students for whom this decision also seemed outrageous. We had attended school, played at parks, ridden public transportation and worked with Blacks all of our lives. Some southern students I admired greatly suddenly seemed bigoted and irrational. True Christians could not speak this way! I knew I could never agree with them. Though I realized they were Christians, I also recognized that these southerners would not easily change their racial attitudes.

It was no wonder either. I chaperoned several student groups who were sent on Christian service assignments to Black churches in the area. These churches were very different from what I was used to. The preaching was not presented in the fashion to which I was accustomed. The audiences spontaneously verbalized their responses to the messages and songs. After I went to Ecuador I realized that my initial responses to Latin American churches had been the same as my reaction to the

Black churches. Today it would be called culture shock. Blacks and Whites lived so separately in the South that lifestyles and responses had to be different.

It was easier to see the social injustice and oppression in Ecuador. I was horrified by the treatment of Indians who made up more than half the total population. They were socially ostracized and did not learn Spanish at all except to trade in the market. They worked as virtual slaves on the large plantations owned by the few rich people in the country. They are paid five cents a day even today and are given a plot of land from which they grow enough food for their own use. Anyone who attempts to do anything about their condition is called a communist. Several American social workers were killed while I was there. Missionaries often were stoned or attacked in some other way when they attempted to present the truth to them. The Ecuadorian establishment would convince the Indians themselves that these very people who wanted to help were actually their enemies.

Along with seeing the social system in Ecuador more objectively than I had in my own country, I was also being greatly influenced by the Bible. I was teaching Bible at the Alliance Seminary in Guayaquil every semester. Over a period of ten years I surveyed the Old and New Testaments a number of times with different students as well as teaching Acts, Romans, Corinthians, Hebrews,

Revelation, Genesis and Joshua analytically. Acts
and the prophetic books became living and real
during those years, and the issue of the church and
social responsibility became more and more important.

It is no wonder than that I found myself much in
sympathy with minority Christian students and
colleagues when I began to teach at Brooklyn
College. When White faculty were invited to attend
the Black faculty meetings, I attended. Only when
the Black faculty gave me a ballot to vote did I
realize that they thought that I too was Black. My
identification with Black students in Inter-Varsity
Christian Fellowship added to the confusion about
my background. After talking with Russ at Urbana,
I decided that unless I was asked directly, I would
not reveal my ethnic background on campus. The
administration often sent forms asking for ethnic
identification, but I refused to say anything about
it. I felt they were asking for unjustifiable reasons.
Paul said he was "all things to all men," and I
take full advantage of the confusion I cause. So in
a world which seems to confuse and yet not to confuse my identity, I have been content as God has
opened doors for relationships and ministry.

The confusion about my ethnic origin thoroughly enmeshed me in the discussions among Black
students at Urbana about their relationships with
Whites and the White Christian world. After the
all-Black sessions the students tried to sort out
their feelings and Christian convictions. I shall

never forget the counseling sessions and rap sessions I had at such times with individuals or small groups of Black students. Emotionally I felt torn apart for I was seeing from the inside the results of our racist society.

I did not feel free to attend meetings which were designed only for Black students. I felt this would be deceitful. However, one day I did walk in on a "closed meeting" and was already seated with Brenda and Jackie before I saw a White student turned away who attempted to attend. I turned to Brenda, who knew my background, and asked her what to do. It seemed embarrassing to leave and yet I felt uneasy about staying. Brenda said, "Stay. It will be good for you."

I did. What I heard was unforgettable. Tom Skinner gave a practical, Scripture-based talk on loving yourself. I'll never forget that talk, nor the sorrow I felt because our dominantly White society made that talk necessary. My admiration for Tom Skinner was greatly enhanced by that experience. My certainty also grew that our Black brethren did indeed need to "get it together" for reasons far different from those many Whites were thinking.

I myself would not even have believed the implication of sociological terms like *alienation* and *depersonalization* had Black students not freely shared with me some of their experiences. At Urbana they expected me to understand because they considered me one of them. Russ told me how as a young teen-ager he had been walking in a White neighborhood when someone had stepped out of a store, glared at him and said, "What are *you* doing in *this* neighborhood?" Bryan would frequently raise his hand in a science class. His teacher always recognized other students, all of whom were White. "It's as if you are transparent; he can't see you." Vince finally quit a part-time job where he had been treated poorly. Glen was another West Indian who poured out his rage because he felt that his Black peers used drugs as an escape from a hostile, dominantly White world.

Melissa, a Black American applying for medical school, had a professor who told her that he simply did not write recommendations for Black students. She decided not to make an issue of this and sought another person. Bryan, however, our president at the time and a proud West Indian, wanted us to go as a club to the department chairman over the issue. I identified with Bryan's reaction, but I first wanted to see the professor personally. Melissa begged us not to do anything. She feared it would arouse the whole department against her. We acquiesced to her wishes. Eventually she was accepted at Rutgers School of Medicine and is doing well there.

Urbana 70 stands out to me in this context for another reason. Karen Lewis, a tall, attractive Jamaican, had been a student in one of my classes. She had responded several months before to my invitation to attend the club. Now she had come along to Urbana. She had come from Jamaica to the United States a few years before, and was naturally very confused and upset at first by the sessions held just for Blacks. I wondered if these sessions were helpful to her at all. Her comprehension of the depth of racial feelings and hurt among Black Americans was limited. My greatest fear was that all of these stirred-up emotions would detract from the spiritual discussions of the conference.

I wish I could say that I was mistaken about this apprehension in every case, but at least I was wrong about Karen. My fear was that deep hostility toward Whites was being created without help also being offered so students could forgive and find solutions. I remember several late-night sessions with Bill Pannell and Tom Skinner when Karen got little sleep. Karen announced that she was determined to find a lifework which would help Black people in the United States. This decision showed that she at least had worked through her feelings. Others in our club did not and are still struggling with this problem.

Then one evening toward the close of the conference Karen came running in and said to me, "Miss B., I have news for you! I just received Christ as my Savior!" I gasped, for I had thought from our previous conversations and her interest in the Word that she had already taken this step at our chapter meetings. She explained that when she left one of the plenary meetings she met a student from

Cornell University Medical School who was from Ghana. They conversed and he asked her very pointedly when she had come to know Christ personally. She could not recall ever having made a commitment; so they prayed together, and now she was radiant. Great relief and joy filled me after all of the previous days of confusion and soul-searching. She called New York to tell her parents and to encourage them to watch the TV coverage of Urbana. This was a highlight in those days of crisis. I wondered how many people were aware even at the conference of how important those days were for all Black students.

I recalled clearly the whole incident a few months later when Karen suddenly had a cerebral hemorrhage. Within twenty-four hours she was with the Lord. The chapter was shocked by this seeming tragedy. We hastened to console her parents. I would have been exceedingly sorrowful myself if it were not for the way her parents accepted her death. Her father welcomed us into their home. He told us of the change which had occurred in Karen's life since she returned from Urbana. He and his wife were sure she was in heaven. He asked us to participate in the funeral service which took place in an all-Black Presbyterian church in the Bushwick area of Brooklyn. The only Whites present at the funeral were her friends from our fellowship. Two of our Black students, Bob and Curt, testified to Karen's life and faith in Christ. We sang several songs we knew she liked, which her parents requested.

Again I have to say how thankful I was for this unforeseen opportunity to give evidence of bonds in Christ which transcend sociological patterns, rules or expectations. I know the people at Karen's church were touched and impressed. Mr. and Mrs. Lewis later advised me that Karen had bequeathed me $100 in her will. I accepted the money but sent it to be used for Urbana scholarships for Black students. The following year the club sent flowers and a note to the parents which they greatly appreciated. We have exchanged Christmas notes each year.

Karen's death provided unusual impetus for breaking through the sociological expectations to a realization of God's expectations for human relations. Our club helped West Indian Christians verbalize more easily their bitterness and disappointments in the United States after having been brought up in dominantly Black societies where they were not seen as different or inferior. It seemed easier for many of them to measure people as individuals rather than as groups and to love even those who did not love them. It is also easier for them to measure objectively their own worth and potential. Our Black American students, however, have a very different background. Through many personal, bitter experiences they know what it is to live all of their lives in an atmosphere pervaded by rejection and alienation.

Some of our second-generation West Indians,

who could understand these feelings as their parents had not been able to, tried to find ways to reach their Black American friends. Glen was concerned but did not experience as much success in reaching out to this group as he would have liked. Later Cheryl, our first female president, spent special time "hanging out" and witnessing on the second floor of SUBO where many Black American students met together socially. We did gradually find a few who were willing to give the fellowship a try. However, until recently we did not have a breakthrough.

The turning point came after I had attended a Tom Skinner banquet with my roommate. During the banquet Skinner told the largely Black, middle-class audience that the only way younger-generation Blacks would give the gospel a hearing was for Blacks to evangelize them. He showed slides of a special effort his organization was making to witness among Black students on predominantly Black campuses. I did not like the implications of what he said. I felt that he was mistaken and that the IVCF chapter at Brooklyn College was a counter-example, a group with some success aside from the use of Black evangelists. I was deeply stirred. I was determined to call Barb Brown, one of our Black IVCF staff members who had been at the banquet, as soon as I got home. Her line was busy and I could not get through.

The next day, still upset, I attended the regular meeting of the executive committee (the leadership of the chapter). I reported my reaction to Skinner's remarks. Most of the committee was Black, and I was suddenly aware that they were strangely quiet!

"What are you thinking?" I asked. Quietly they told me that Tom was right!

"Well," I said, "why aren't you doing something about it?" Of course I knew that they were doing something on a one-to-one level, but I felt they should have realized it would take more than that to penetrate the group as a whole. They explained that they had been hesitant because they knew our orientation toward integration. They felt that they might be misunderstood.

The outcome of further discussion was a decision to have a special outreach directed toward Black Americans. We held the first outreach of this type in the spring of that school year. We were nervous, so we relied heavily on Soul Liberation, the same Black music group with which we had traveled to Urbana 70. We had to exercise some faith for the finances, but the Lord provided this through sacrifices within the club and support of friends outside.

This outreach took place in the Penthouse, a spacious area located on the sixth floor of SUBO. It could hold up to six hundred students. Doreen, a tall, bright Aruban student, and destined to become a staffer for IVCF, was organizing the refreshments in the kitchen. The White woman responsible for service had an aversion to Black groups and was obviously giving Doreen a hard time. Doreen finally spoke to me about this. I told the woman that Doreen was the authorized person to tell her when and how refreshments were to be served. She did as Doreen directed without further problems. Dexter, the Chinese action group leader, and Mike, an Italian executive committee member, were quietly setting up the literature tables in the back. Our Black members were sitting in the audience with their classmates and friends. Bryan, our West Indian president, gave the introductory remarks.

Soul Liberation was tremendous. Using their music they gradually got into a message of love, very low-keyed and informal. They closed with the greatest love story there ever was: Jesus Christ dying for sinners. No one walked out. The head of Soul Liberation dared anyone to stand up and indicate that he or she wanted to know this love and this Jesus. Just one student stood up. He then walked right up to the front. We invited people to stay for refreshments and rapping. At least fifty students stayed and our Black Christians had an hour to rap. Several decisions were made to accept Christ. Others started attending chapter meetings regularly to check us out. The White employee apologized, saying that she hadn't known what we were wanting to do. Doreen smiled knowingly and gave her a gospel portion.

It is impossible to say all that this meeting meant to the club. Never in our previous outreaches had we seen such openness to the message. It was obvious which direction we were to take in the following year. Since this first outreach we have had other Black outreaches which confirmed Tom Skinner's observation that, though not the only way, it is best on campuses to have Blacks evangelize Blacks. I hated to admit it, but we had to follow the sociological theory and work from there as a starting point.

5

To the Jew First

Having talked so much about the other minority groups on campus, I would not blame my readers for wondering what contacts, if any, we had with Jewish students. After all, they represented by far the largest portion of the student body.

We always felt a responsibility to evangelize our Jewish friends. The Scriptures say, "to the Jew first and also to the Gentile." We did want to be true to the spirit of these words. Some students, like Thelma and Albert (an Egyptian), held evangelistic Bible studies on campus with Jewish classmates. This was done more easily in the daytime session because many of these Jews were "secular" Jews, that is, their families did not practice any religion in their homes. They either did not attend any temple at all, or they were members of liberal reformed temples. Their beliefs were like those of liberal, humanistic Christian institutions.

These secular Jewish students occasionally came to our special topical discussions. For example, a good many attended when Dr. Bolton Davidheiser presented a Christian view of evolution. Strong debate followed his presentation, but few of the students returned to our regular meetings.

We also tried to reach orthodox Jews by having good literature on our booktable which examined the Scriptures and reasoned about Jesus as Messiah. This literature was picked up and read by a number of our friends. Occasionally some Jewish student would return for further discussion, but this was not often. Most orthodox Jews did not like to be seen near our table, much less dialoging with us in public. We discovered that this forum for biblical discussion was not permitted in some orthodox circles. Jews had no dealings with Gentiles.

On two occasions we did show *His Land,* a beautiful film on Israel put out by the Billy Graham Association. We advertised in the school newspapers and put up posters on campus. We used the bullhorn around the quadrangle for further publicity on the day of the showing.

These presentations were well attended, especially by orthodox Jews. I was amazed because they respectfully remained until the end of the film. Much fulfilled prophecy which concerns Israel and Jesus, the Messiah, is given toward the end. On both occasions we also were able to give out some literature. However, we saw little if any visible results in changed beliefs.

I had been also pleased by the openness of some of the Jewish students to Os Guinness when he visited our campus. I asked him to address my classes on the contemporary human dilemma. Guinness presented a historical and philosophical development in which he dealt with the events and ideas leading up to our modern maladies. Later, I realized they were part of his preparations for writing *The Dust of Death*. Then, as I had hoped, questions were raised about possible solutions. Guinness called for a reasoned investigation and evaluation of traditional Judeo-Christianity.

Recent trends make me realize that Guinness's viewpoints would have been more appreciated after the Vietnam War. Students today are in a less emotional and more reflective state of mind, and are more ready and willing to follow a reasoned argument. His penetrating questions went over most of my students' heads at the time. I do not think that would happen today. Nevertheless, even then, a few students did listen and did express appreciation for the exposure to his particular point of view.

In the meantime, Thelma DeVine joined the

campus drive for Soviet Jewry, and she and several other members at different times have taken courses in Judaic studies. These classes were profitable to them historically and biblically. They also provided them with opportunities in class discussion and in papers to express their Christian views concerning God's purpose and plan for the Jews of the world. As a club we also contributed toward the United Jewish Fund drive which seeks to help needy Jews.

Throughout the years of our "reactivation" (1969-77) we always had some Hebrew Christian members in our club. They never represented a large number, but they have always been there. New Christians sometimes did not stay long. The intense opposition on campus to their stand for Christ frightened them. They sometimes chose to attend church or supportive Bible studies off campus. Others, however, were willing to face the antagonism and be faithful despite the problems.

During the year of our concentrated effort to evangelize the Jews we had more Hebrew Christians than ever before. Some of the concern in the club to tell Jewish students about Christ initiated with them. At least six Hebrew Christians were part of our evening fellowship. There were three or four in our day club.

Two people in particular in 1972-73 pushed us into more aggressive evangelism among Jews. It is only natural that we should have come in contact with Art Katz (author of *The Odyssey of a Modern*

Jew) and Moishe Rosen (leader of Jews for Jesus). Both are interested in Jewish evangelism; both could see the advantage Inter-Varsity had as a chartered club on a predominantly Jewish campus; both knew that young Jews are more open than their parents to considering the claims of Jesus Christ. Both individuals are considered radical among Hebrew Christians. Some Hebrew Christians felt that these two men were using confrontation tactics which copy the world. They felt that those approaches might be more alienating than attracting.

Katz, during his visit to us, reprimanded us sharply and firmly, though kindly, for not knowing the Old Testament better and for not being more willing to pointedly discuss issues which would inevitably arouse the Jewish community. Moishe Rosen's influence was less direct. He never visited our campus; if we had invited him, there would have been violence. It would also have stirred up animosity for some time. Moishe did understand our difficulty, but he too insisted directly and indirectly that we really should be more willing to employ confrontation. We were also in contact with local Christians who work among the Jews and were anxious to provide literature. We were selective, looking for the most appropriate and scriptural pieces for our table.

One Christmas, after our usual caroling all over campus, we gave out about five thousand broadsides (tracts from Jews for Jesus) which related

Christmas to Jesus the Messiah. Our caroling had been well received, but in the middle of the distribution of these broadsides we were stopped by school authorities because we had failed to identify ourselves on the back of the literature. I simply told our members, "Well, stamp them and keep going." It did not occur to me at first that on previous occasions we had distributed, without hindrance, other literature which had not been stamped. A few days later the dean of student affairs called to tell me that these tracts were indeed in poor taste. I did not know it at the time, but this was the first of a series of subtle efforts to deter freedom of expression.

We had had a number of sessions on how to evangelize Jews and had studied the prophets. We felt we were ready to attempt more open outreach on campus. I must admit I was a bit apprehensive during this time. I felt certain we were going to have difficulties, but I did not feel we should be deterred by the potential problems if there was a general openness on the part of Jews to the gospel. A number of reports from Hebrew Christian organizations indicated that this was a particularly receptive time for Jewish evangelism.

From this point on I cannot recall the chronology of a number of events which followed one after the other. I received a series of calls and letters from Dean MacGregor telling me that the club was a fine group, that they were an unusual group of students, that they were the only ones who inte-

grated racially with success, but that we were step-
ping over the line if we were going to proselytize
among Jews. This was a violation of church and
state. After all, Brooklyn College was a public institution, wasn't it? (I must confess that I do not
know why our evangelism was not a violation of
the rights of Black Muslims or atheists or human-
ists or the gay groups on campus!)

The dean expressed surprise that our educated
students could be so narrow-minded that they believed that Jews also needed to believe in Jesus
Christ. In good humanistic tradition we ought to
dialog about our differences and let it go at that.
Surely we did not think that Jews needed to be con-
verted! Why, just look at all of the needs of the
non-Jews on campus! (A gentle slur to remind us
that the other minority students were far less law-
abiding!) I remember conversing several times
with Dean MacGregor, who impressed me as being
an opportunist. He also sent me an article written
by a large, modern denomination which derided
the Key 73 evangelism of Jews, and assured me
that he had great faith in my intelligence and per-
ception of the issues.

Then he sent me another letter, telling me that
Vice President Gold had been advised that IVCF
students were "buttonholing" Jews in order to tell
them about Jesus. In the chapter we had previously
discussed some specific ground rules for evangelism at the table. There was to be discussion only
with those who wanted to dialog. No one was to

raise his or her voice or argue, even if the other party did. It was better to lose an argument than to lose a friend! We were all going to be very careful not to touch anyone else so that it could never be misconstrued.

I must admit that I was angry when I got the last note. It was the culmination of a series which constantly warned us that we were out of line, rocking the boat and were, of course, always wrong—even if it was our students who were incited by defensive Jews. I was also adamant in my defense of the chapter because the dean refused to give me the names of any students who had committed these crimes, nor would he say that he himself had seen these things happen. He did say that some students had tried to convert him when he approached the table—and that he did *not* like! When I suggested that the complainants confront the officers of our club, he was reluctant.

I became aware through these phone calls, letters and personal conversations that the dean was under heavy pressure from upstairs. Rabbi Fischer, the sponsor of the campus Hillel Club, and Hilary Gold, the vice president of Brooklyn College, were getting carbon copies of the correspondence he sent me. Powerful forces, which were trying to stay out of sight, were bearing down on him, and he felt it necessary to respond. I finally decided to answer with carbon copies not only to Vice President Gold and Rabbi Fischer but also to President Kneller and Father Brown of the Newman Club.

It was the spring of 1973 and the entire Jewish community was aroused. There were, of course, many outside reasons for their alarm. Israel was struggling to maintain its position in the Middle East while the Arabs pressured Europe and the United States with the oil embargo. The Israeli athletes had been killed in Munich the previous fall. The recent recession in New York City had brought fear and unrest about employment. The future did not seem bright for the Jewish community. Many parents and grandparents were recalling to their children the Nazi experience. This was evident from class discussions and the school newspapers. At the same time, the Young Socialists, made up largely of secular Jews, had invited an Arab to speak about the injustices being perpetuated by Israel against the Palestinian refugees. They had had to call the police to prevent a major confrontation with Zionist Jews.

With this in mind I felt divided about aggressive evangelism. I knew that we were being sincerely misunderstood by some and deliberately misinterpreted by others. How should we proceed? All I could do was pray for God's guidance.

6

Opposition and Coalition

The increased number of Hebrew Christians in the chapter was a factor in the rising opposition we experienced. Our deliberate attempt to become more visible certainly contributed. In any case, the greatest opposition came in the evenings. More orthodox and zealous Jews attended Brooklyn College in the evening. The evangelism table was set up in Whitehead Building once a week. It became apparent that more and more Jews deliberately antagonized our Hebrew Christians who worked the table. The latter did not seem to mind too much but rather used the jibes and vilification as opportunities to witness.

Then attempts were made to steal our boxes of

literature, sometimes successfully. The literature was ransacked in my office. Graffiti was painted on the walls in an attempt to discourage us. Art Goyena, back at Brooklyn College for graduate study, lost Bibles and books along with the literature on several occasions. One night I arrived at Whitehead just in time to see a box being stolen from under the booktable while large handfuls of tracts were being lifted from the table itself. Art was exasperated after his previous experiences and went tearing after the fellow with the box. I knew from the familiar faces that they really wanted Art to give them an excuse to fight.

I ran after Art, grabbed his sports jacket and said, "Art, it is not worth it! Let them take it!"

He stopped, took a deep breath, looked at me and said, "You're right, Miss B. I'm sorry. Guess I lost my cool."

Several others came over to try to upset Art with words, but he did not succumb. God was with us, thanks to the prayers of many Christians whom we had called.

Then I walked to the exit of the building and saw the tracts and booklets strewn across the street which separated Whitehead Building from the Student Building. I began to pick up the hundreds of tracts which were thrown all over. As I did so, several unknown students, also Jewish, came by and helped me.

"How did this stuff get here?" they asked. I explained how the JDL students had taken the literature.

They were angry.

"They have no right to do this."

I asked if they would accompany me to the evening dean of students, Dr. Bigel, to make a formal complaint. They seemed to know more about the actual culprits and they acquiesced. We went to the dean's office. The dean took note of the event. A formal complaint was to be made, but it was obvious that Dr. Bigel felt that we had brought the problem on ourselves.

Months before all these problems hit us, we had invited Dr. Rachmiel Frydland, a learned Hebrew Christian, to speak on campus. He had endured cruel treatment in Poland during the Nazi reign because some Christians were afraid to protect him at times. He spoke both Hebrew and Yiddish. We thought that his sympathetic views toward Israel and his background would allow him to be heard by our Jewish friends. Having made these plans with the approval of the IVCF staff member, we went ahead with the publicity.

Dean MacGregor called again. Rabbi Fischer wanted to see me, he said. Could Jack, our president, and I meet in his office? I wondered why Rabbi Fischer had not called himself and why the dean felt we had to have the meeting in his office. I called Jack and we prayed.

When we got to the dean's office, the Rabbi never appeared. The dean called him, and we were told that he had been unavoidably detained. He could see us in the afternoon at the Hillel Club building just off campus.

I will never forget that meeting. The rabbi called his president when he saw that Jack still accompanied me. He inquired about our activities with regard to Jews. He especially pointed out how upset the Jewish community was by the movement called Jews for Jesus. There was obvious concern for their young people. He felt that the broadsides were insulting to Jewish culture and gave me examples of this. He claimed that we were being used, unsuspectingly of course, by outside sources to penetrate the campus with ideas which were totally unacceptable to the Jews. I gasped, gulped and then asked to see the material to which he was referring. He had only one broadside which made only one cultural jibe, and it was obviously done jokingly, not intended to insult. It was clear that the broadside had been written by a Jew.

I too decided to ask some questions. Couldn't Hillel Club offer some good teaching about God and about values which Judaism was not now emphasizing? Wouldn't this be better than to encroach on the freedom of another group to express its views? I also reminded him that conservative Christians with views which our club represented were pro-Israel, were not anti-Semitic and were sympathetic to those whom the Bible says have a particular place in history.

He finally said to us that the only possible way

for IVCF and Hillel or any other Jewish group to live together amicably was for IVCF to remove from the evangelism table all literature with a particular message for Jews. This he felt was absolutely necessary. We reminded him that we not only had literature on the table for Jews but also for Blacks, Puerto Ricans and women besides all the books and booklets which are directed toward humanist, agnostic and atheistic students. We also told him that if we did not evangelize Jews we could not be Christians. The injunction in the New Testament is to evangelize all people, the Jews first and then the Gentiles. I reminded him that Brooklyn College was not a Yeshiva (a Jewish parochial school) but a public institution.

He was upset and finally told us that he would be unable to control or stop the JDL from any measures against us if we would not listen to reason. I was shocked. No wonder he had asked us to go to his office! He never could have said this in front of Dean MacGregor. I replied that I could not worry about this problem. It was his, not ours.

"We have been on this campus for four years now. We are not known to be violent—rather to be pacific and lovers and makers of peace. At the same time we do believe we have the right to express ourselves even if our beliefs are contrary to or different from the dominant group on the campus. Minority groups do have rights. If you think that by violence you can disgrace or hurt us, you are greatly mistaken. The ones who will be answerable will be the Jews, not just the JDL, for it will be obvious that the community approves their action since it is not stopping them."

I was concerned when we left his office. I had read in the newspapers about the actions of the JDL. I was worried about the safety of the students for whom I felt responsible. It was easy to be bold in front of the rabbi. It was another story when it came to confronting the reality of possible acts of reprisal.

We decided not to cancel the meeting with Dr. Frydland. We continued to advertise the event. We had secured Breuklen Lounge, one of the larger rooms in the Student Building, for the occasion. I was teaching until the hour of the meeting. Several of my own students were there when I arrived. I had told my "Bible As Literature" students about the speaker, in case any were interested. A good number of the Inter-Varsity students were there too, both from the day and evening chapters. Even more exciting was the fact that Cliff, a Jewish believer who came to Christ during his undergraduate years at another college, had brought his father to hear the speaker. The room was quite full of Jewish students and some adults. Rabbi Fisher was also there but he left early. At first I was pleased but I did not remain pleased for long.

John Calderone came to me anxiously. He was the leader of the evening club this term. "Miss B., they will not allow us to begin our meeting. They insist that Dr. Frydland cannot speak!" I was amazed! If they had jeered while the speaker addressed the group, I would have been less surprised. The JDL leader, a former student government officer who had been expelled for illicit actions, stood up and began to speak loudly.

"One moment," I said, "this meeting was called by Inter-Varsity Christian Fellowship. We have every right to have the speaker of our choice. No one has to attend this meeting if they would prefer not to."

"No," came the reply. "This man is out to kill the souls of our Jewish brothers and sisters. We will not allow him to do that."

Then it dawned on me why there was such a large representation of Jewish adults. There were several rabbis from the Anti-Missionary Association who wished to convince the Hebrew Christians of the error of their way. The Jewish Defense League was there in full force. I had read *Never Again* and knew we could not contend with their fascist tactics and arguments. I left the room to get help from the authorities!

When I got to the office I found that the only person there was Mr. Serapski, a Jewish man with whom some of our students had spoken when making plans for special events in the building. He was rather new in the position, and I was dubious about his ability to deal with the situation. At any rate, I requested that he expel the individuals who were causing the problem and that we be allowed to continue our program.

"Miss Benjamin," he said, "there is no way to stop *them!*"

From our conversation I realized that the leader was known in the Jewish community for his ability to create turmoil wherever he chose. Mr. Serapski accompanied me upstairs and asked the leaders to leave. By this time the air was tense. Accusations were shouted. He could do nothing with them. The IVCF students had taken out their Bibles and were discussing their beliefs with the JDL students. The speaker was addressing several around him. I decided to see if I could isolate the leaders while the students shared their Christian beliefs and faith. I have never had so many hateful words directed to me. I recognized the same irrational arguments used against Jews on previous occasions.

"How can you do to others," I asked, "what you would not, did not, want done to yourselves?" The next hour and a half was filled with words which were later sent by the JDL in a letter to the editor of the school newspaper. We were accused of being like the Nazis. The only difference was that we Christians were organized to destroy the souls of Jews instead of their bodies. If we would not listen to their warnings we deserved not only to be boycotted but to be stopped in any possible way.

At the end of two hours I saw that Dr. Frydland was continuing to answer questions while one young Jewish Defense Leaguer screamed at him. I turned to Jack, president of the day group, and said, "Get that poor man out of here. Make sure that no one follows him. Take him home." Jack and several others accompanied Dr. Frydland to the car while the JDL students gave him their final insults. With a sigh of relief, full of anxiety and nervous tension, I too was driven home.

I was not there, but the students told me that Dr. Whipple, director of the Student Building, came to their meeting the next day and formally apologized for the interruption of the conference the previous night. The leader of the group was deprived of his privileges to enter the building for a month.

Good relations and good testimony do pay off, for Dr. Whipple has always respected the club and has gladly given us a fair opportunity to use the various lounges. We knew that he had frequent problems with property damage, drugs, alcoholism and so on. Inter-Varsity had tried to be careful about its relations with others and with the care of property. When Inter-Varsity's multimedia ministry, TWENTYONEHUNDRED, visited campus, Dr. Whipple had seen their equipment first-hand as well as the care with which the club treated all the operations. In fact, the presentation of TWENTYONEHUNDRED had been a testimony from beginning to end because of the care given to property and equipment and the courtesy shown to all of the employees of the Student Building. The college communications department had also been impressed with the presentation itself, and this gave us more visibility and possibility of witness. Today, one Jewish technician to whom several of us, especially Cheryl, had witnessed is a Hebrew Christian. He and his wife attend a small church near the campus.

The weekend after the meeting with Dr. Frydland I was to assist Conrad Sauer with teaching and leading a small group Bible study at an IVCF training conference. I was an emotional wreck and did not want to go. I knew I would not be any better at home, so I went anyway. I shared with the group there what had happened to us, but I was unable to unwind or to tell anyone the impact it had had on me. Somehow I made it through the weekend. The Lord made it possible for Conrad to drive me to the city. On the way I unloaded all my fears and anxieties. I was able to have a good cry which released pent-up feelings. Conrad was sympathetic and promised to support me any time I needed it. He also prayed with me before I took the subway home.

I will always be grateful to Conrad for that helpful moment. Until that time I had felt very alone and very responsible for the chapter. From time to time I had met to pray with various Christian faculty, but the meetings were never consistent because of changing schedules and the fact that all of us lived off campus. Club hours often conflicted with faculty meetings or other professional obligations, so we could not meet easily to pray at those times either. In fact, I never have been able to find faculty who would give priority to prayer or to the needs of a corporate witness on campus. I do not want to **appear to blame or condemn.** Many of them were already totally committed to their families, professions and churches. There were many demands on them. However, at this particular time, when I felt the need for faculty support and understanding, there was none.

As a result of my time with Conrad I realized not just mentally but experientially that I was not alone, that God was with me and that he wanted me to lean on others for support. I had a deeper sense of the importance of developing a relationship with IVCF staff and other Christian faculty. I had always relied on Hephzibah House for prayer support. Now God was leading into a closer tie with IVCF staff. Before this time, Conrad had occasionally been out to the college, but he was covering a large number of other campuses at the same time. For obvious reasons the visits were infrequent.

After this, however, Conrad began calling regularly to ask how things were going and came to the college whenever I asked for his counsel and presence. It was immensely helpful, giving me courage to cope with the situation and support whenever the club and I were asked to visit the office of the dean of student activities. In fact, as I formally introduced Conrad to the dean, I realized that the college was viewing us as if we were strange and wondrous Jesus freaks. They did not know the history and tradition Inter-Varsity has had on many campuses throughout our nation and throughout the world. Conrad gave literature describing IVCF to the dean. He, in turn, communicated this to the lawyer of the college who at that time, unbeknownst to us, was seeking to accumulate sufficient evidence to uncharter the club. The possible allegations against us were anti-Semitism and/or proselytizing.

This was not our only problem. The student government that year was made up largely of orthodox and conservative Jews who, under the influence of the JDL and their understandably paranoid parents and community, had decided to prosecute us through the student court. This was 1973 and many Jews had been warned by their synagogues about Key 73 evangelism. They were sure that IVCF was a front organization for Jews for Jesus as well as for Key 73. This had been made clear at the meeting with Rabbi Fischer. (The administration could have helped to avoid this problem by allowing Hebrew Christians their right of expression through the Jews for Jesus organization. This, of course, was out of the question!)

As we prayed about our problems, I felt intuitively that we had to do something to gain some visibility if the college was ever to get a perspective that was true and fair. I called Conrad and suggested that we invite some community people, both clergy and laity, to meet with the dean to express concern about the loss of freedom of speech at the college. Conrad sent me a list of names of local clergy. I added names of those I knew. Other names came through the members of the club. A formal letter was sent to each one. I called a number of them and explained more fully the need for their presence. Many of the contacts had no idea that it was so difficult to present the gospel on the campus. They expressed interest and willingness to support us. A number accepted the invitation to the meeting with the dean.

In addition to the fine group of evangelical ministers and lay people who supported us, God raised up others. One was Rev. Thompson, the minister of the United Methodist Church near the college. Several of our club members attended his church which had always been helpful. The pastor was well known in the area and had experience with confrontation tactics during the social action era of the late sixties. In fact, his staunch support for us stemmed from his disillusionment with previous efforts to solve our nation's problems. He had seen the transformation and new motivation in the members of his church. Thelma and Ginnie, who both became Christians through the chapter, had begun attending and had helped others to make personal commitments to Christ. They formed the DugOut Coffee House to help many drug addicts in the area.

Another supporter was Father Alden Brown of the Newman Club. IVCF had formal interaction with the Newman Center at least once a semester. I had lunch with Father Brown and his assistant occasionally too. Father Brown did not feel that the college had a right to prevent the club from expressing its views, even though he himself differed with us at some points.

Another man who was helpful to us was Professor Alexander Barton. He was a leader in one of the largest and most influential black churches in Brooklyn. In addition, he was an administrator in the evening program at Brooklyn College. I had met him quite accidentally in the Student Building where he expressed appreciation for the club. When I went to his office to explain the problem, he was enraged. When the dean tried to explain to him about our efforts to evangelize Jews, he simply said, "That is what the Bible says to do!" Professor Barton was an enigma to me because I knew that he had graduated from a liberal theological seminary and that some people felt that the church he attended was not very evangelical. He had never attended our club meetings, probably because the majority of them were held during the day. Yet I certainly appreciated his West Indian sense of propriety and his keen sense of justice. I am sure that he spoke out because he felt our black students needed support. Thus God raised up people in his own way. Prayer had been the key to knowing what to do and in making the right contacts.

Another individual who would have come to

our aid if I had asked him was Meyer Cantor, the faculty sponsor of the Young Socialists. He felt that I was not aggressive enough with the authorities. Meyer himself was Jewish, but he had no patience with the arbitrary and one-sided views of the right-wing Jews. I feared that we would lose all opportunity to witness to this dominant right-wing segment if we permitted Meyer to be a part of this group.

God was with us the day we met with the dean of student affairs. Professor Barton had secured the office of the dean of evening studies for the meeting. Rev. Thompson took the lead in asking for an explanation for the various problems the club was having. Why was the table not being protected by security guards at the school? How could an invited speaker be prevented from giving his talk in a public institution? Where were the authorities when they knew the tensions existed? Since when were minority rights not respected? Rev. Thompson was quite adamant. For the first time the dean was defensive. Mr. Scacalossi, the security chief for the school, was summoned. He promised to have his guards on hand in the future. We were to advise his office of times and places for our public meetings. I was proud of the way our club officers refused to allow anyone to misinterpret the facts as they were discussed. It was more than noticeable that Rabbi Fischer did not appear, even though he had been requested to attend. I was grateful for each one who came at our request. God was using this to help them understand the spiritual need of the secular university. He was answering prayer more than I had ever dreamed.

It was not long after this meeting that the dean sent me another letter, informing me that the opinion of the attorneys of the college was that the literature distributed by the club was "not to be considered an attack on a religion within the framework of the Bylaws." The dean also said that he "was not comfortable with this interpretation. Nevertheless, the college would put forward all necessary effort to secure the rights of free expression of all students including the use of whatever security measures were required."

As I read this letter I realized why I had been so burdened. I had no idea until then that the lawyer had been investigating our club's activities and literature. No wonder I had felt such concern. I thanked God for his discretion and guidance.

Still pending was the matter of the student government court case. The semester was drawing to a close, and we still did not know what the charges were. We supposed from letters and articles in *Kingsman*, the official campus newspaper, that it would be anti-Semitism, but we had no formal correspondence to confirm this. The executive committee tried to get more information—but without success. The dean, in a friendly tone, advised me to wait it out.

Just as classes were ending, IVCF was notified to appear before the student government. I was chagrined because I knew our executive committee needed time to study for final exams. We went to the first appointed meeting, and no one from the student government showed up. Then we were given a second date. This date was during final exams. I was worried, not only because it was exam time but because I knew that if we were unjustly treated, there would be no way to communicate this to the public. The last edition of the school newspaper had been printed for the term, and students do not get excited about any issue during exam time.

I went to the dean and told him that I felt that the timing was totally inappropriate. He agreed and promised to do what he could. A few days later he called to tell me that the charges had been dropped. We could continue as a regularly chartered club on campus. We all thanked God for the way he had intervened all year long. He had given wisdom when needed, enabled us to clarify our witness for Christ through the problems caused, raised up supporters when needed and prevented the intentions of evildoers from being realized—and through it all he had enabled us to walk and talk as Christians who had no reason to be ashamed.

7

Being Fully Known

The Inter-Varsity chapter often felt tension with the faculty and administration. It was all the more important, then, that the college officials have a clear, objective view of who we were and of what our purposes were on campus. We had been viewed for some time as a front organization for Jews for Jesus. Inter-Varsity Christian Fellowship with its history of Christian ministry on hundreds of campuses in the United States and abroad was unknown at Brooklyn College. Some of the paranoia about us could be quelled by a simple presentation of ourselves as a legitimate worldwide movement.

Eventually we hit upon the idea of a faculty tea.

We would invite every administrator and professor and many community leaders to a program of refreshments, song, testimonies and a main speaker. The Newman Club and Hillel had annual faculty teas. We decided to have ours in the afternoon from 4:00 to 6:00. These hours were selected because daytime faculty could stay and attend; evening faculty could come just a bit earlier. In addition, pastors and community people would find these hours convenient. Those who worked could get permission to leave their jobs a little earlier or simply come a little late. So what began as a technique to gain greater visibility within the university establishment also became another vehicle for evangelism.

The students took full responsibility for this ministry. The project was assigned to a small committee who in turn assigned various facets of the tea to the proper action groups. Letters were sent to every administrator from the president of the college on down. Two of the club officers, dressing neatly and somewhat more formally than usual, hand delivered these letters. They would ask the secretary in each department to see the administrator. If this was not possible, they explained the purpose of their visit, delivered the letter and asked for a written reply to be sent to me, the faculty sponsor. The letter itself was signed by the president of the club and by myself. My signature was not necessary, but we thought it would be helpful.

We made special visits to invite the dean of student affairs. I accompanied the club president. Through the dean's office we pressed for the presence of the college president. If he could attend Newman Club functions and never fail to be at the Hillel programs, why should he ignore us?

In addition we sent announcements to the faculty, each member receiving an invitation in his or her mailbox at least three weeks ahead of time. At Brooklyn College this meant about two thousand letters. The publicity action group composed the invitation and had it printed. They personally distributed these to the various departments, requesting permission to put them in the boxes. Sometimes the secretaries were glad to let them do it. Other times the secretaries promised to distribute them. Our students learned to deal courteously and patiently with the various departments. In this way IVCF was a common name on the campus within a few years.

As well as putting the formal invitations into the boxes, we wrote letters to the current professors of our members. These were again drafted with great care by the secretary. Again we used national Inter-Varsity Christian Fellowship letterhead, and again the president and faculty sponsor signed the letters. These letters were given to each member of the group; they in turn personally gave their professors a verbal and written invitation to the tea. Letters of invitation were also extended to the counselors and staff at the Learning Center and counseling offices. We found that many of the people who attended the tea came as a result of personal contacts.

I felt responsible to invite my colleagues to these teas. Many of them already knew about my sponsorship of the club. I had a number of good friends in the School of Education. I had worked on committees or team-taught with them. Throughout the years I had sought to present the claims of the gospel to them. After some discussions on school matters or other issues, I looked for appropriate Christian books to give or lend them. As the date for the tea approached, I gave them the invitations when I met them in the halls or at meetings. I wrote a personal note on the invitations which went in their mailboxes. Then about a week before the reception I sent a gentle reminder.

Besides the faculty and administration, we also invited the community. At first our community was the group who came to protest the encroachment of our rights of speech and association in 1973. Later we added the names of other pastors, alumni and interested friends. We thought that the combination was ideal. Administrators would feel a stronger obligation to be there when they knew the faculty would be there. Community friends could talk with administrators and faculty and tell them how important they felt the club was to them. In view of the Jewish opposition we were receiving, this seemed extremely important.

No matter how tense I was, the club planned

and presented the program. And in the first years I was *very* nervous. After that I was just nervous! I wanted everything to be right. The students made a great effort to have the best presentation. The girls wore dresses, sometimes long dresses if they were serving, and the fellows wore suits. They spent hours practicing appropriate songs. They themselves prepared and brought the refreshments.

In the spring of 1976 we had an unexpected disruption of the school calendar because of the crisis in city finances. The issue was the discontinuance of open admissions. Further education for the lower classes was being frustrated at the City University, the institution which was created for this reason. There was a great reduction in funds available to help students who had attended schools which prepared them inadequately for college. Several colleges which were Black and Puerto Rican were being closed or limited. Medgar Evers, a predominantly Black, four-year college, was threatened with becoming a two-year community college. Its nursing and other professional training programs might also be cut. Hostos Community College, a bilingual two-year college in the Bronx was to be discontinued.

We invited Dr. R. Loney, then chairman of the education department at Medgar Evers, to speak from a Christian perspective about these sudden changes. We felt Dr. Loney's position in the City University would attract attention among the faculty and administration. In addition, as a Black faculty member involved in a church in Harlem, he would greatly help our minority students to see their roles as future Christian leaders.

When I called him to confirm the club's written invitation, he asked me if I had to know ahead of time what he would say. Dr. Loney had reason to ask. He had doubts that IVCF, a WASPy organization, could identify with Black urban problems. He had strong feelings about the abrupt closing of opportunities for upward mobility among minority groups. I assured him that our students especially would want to know any solutions or actions they should take. We wanted the faculty and community to know our concerns.

It was a great meeting. Even though our dates had been disrupted and notices had been late, we had a good turnout. Dr. Loney was a verbal man. He described some of his participation in civil rights and social justice issues. He spoke vividly of some embittering experiences in the South which reminded me of John Perkins's books, *Let Justice Roll Down* and *A Quiet Revolution*. He also told us how in the years of struggling for the rights of Blacks he had learned that bitterness and hatred were not the answer. Forgiveness through Christ and love were the liberating forces for taking positive action. The church could be the channel for these forces, meeting human needs—social, emotional, intellectual. As an educator, Dr. Loney had grasped how important it was to tutor disadvantaged children. He recognized that the church could have an important role in teaching children not only the mechanics of the three Rs but the moral values they sorely lacked.

The club was quickened by Dr. Loney's talk. Dean McGregor was impressed and joined in the discussion of the proper steps and action we could take. One strong conviction came to some of us. We must begin to work to encourage tutoring programs in our urban evangelical churches. For growing as Christians means absorbing God's Word, and reading and writing are integral to this. Before we can understand God and his will for our lives, we must be able to read well enough to study his Word. This had become clear to me in Ecuador when I tried to help adult Christians grow spiritually. I came to realize that they were limited by their barely functional literacy. Conrad and I began to make plans for a pilot program during the coming summer. These efforts are examined in the next chapter.

Knowing the value of having an outside speaker who was able to deal with a current topic, we began to look for someone to speak at our next faculty tea. We also saw the need for a speaker whom the faculty and administration could respect. There was a sense of cynicism and demoralization on campus. People had talked about problems for so long, yet there seemed to be no solutions. There was a growing paralysis of free thinking which was heightened by the loss of employment and irrational bureaucratic practices. No one was addressing the deep crises of values our society faced.

We decided to invite Dr. Leon Stamatis, a surgeon and an associate professor at Down State Medical School to be our speaker. Dr. Stamatis discussed these issues with me and then began to do some serious reading on the matter. "Confronting a Monolithic Society" was the title we decided on. Vince, our president, liked it, so we went ahead. Dr. Stamatis was acquainted with Dr. Francis Schaeffer's analysis of contemporary Western culture. I later gave him a copy of *How Should We Then Live?* for his kindnesses to us.

We also invited Sydney Johnson to sing. He was a well-known voice instructor in the music department and our students admired him both as a Christian and as a professional. The combination of a Greek surgeon and a Black musician surely would make an interesting faculty tea.

I never dreamed, though, that we would have such a fine turnout. Each year I was delighted by the number of responses I got personally. My chairman came on two occasions and showed great interest in the club, and my colleagues in teamteaching were very responsive to my invitations. Several of the administrators came, some of whom were my friends and whom I knew had genuine concern about the problems of our society and our college. I could share with the students their satisfaction and joy when their teachers came too. I was especially pleased at the number of Black staff who took an interest in our club for the first time. In addition, many committed laymen and local pastors came with their wives.

As usual, I was everywhere and nowhere. Evelina told me to sit down and relax when I told the students that they ought to mix more with the group. I wanted everything to be perfect. I should have known that our guests would simply be pleased to see the students be themselves and speak from their hearts. Will I never learn?

During the informal time before the program began Conrad showed a multimedia presentation about the national Inter-Varsity movement. We projected this at one end of a large room ideal for an elegant reception. People could casually interact or watch as they chose. Materials were displayed which would help all to understand IVCF. We also made available IVP booklets which introduce the gospel and put out some books which dealt with the talk to be given. Sandwiches, snacks, punch, tea and coffee were served by the students. I did my usual flitting here and there, despite the admonitions to relax, never quite deciding where I wanted to be most, to chat with friends, colleagues or the students' teachers, alumni or pastors.

The students opened the formal part of the tea with songs. Paul Roberts, a Hebrew Christian senior, gave a testimony. Vince, the president, did a great job as master of ceremonies. All of the students were aware of their roles. The program committee had the main responsibility while the fellowship action group watched to see that there were enough refreshments. While the students ran many of our informal events more casually, they knew what was expected by this professional audience, and they did not miss a thing.

I was asked to give the usual greeting from the faculty sponsor. How easily words can come when one is proud and happy! But wait a minute, there was something I did not expect. The president was talking about me still, taking longer than usual, and before I knew it, I had been given a lovely orchid corsage by Evelina, our secretary. I was surprised—and pleased.

Sydney Johnson sang superbly and in good taste —one classical number and then a Negro spiritual, "Sweet Little Jesus Boy," just before Dr. Stamatis spoke. I could tell that the Lord had led Dr. Stamatis to use some thoughts which came from Clark Pinnock and Francis Schaeffer. His extended closing remarks, however, were clearly from John Stott's *Basic Christianity* and were a defense of belief in the resurrection of Jesus Christ. He had given the true picture of our broken world, of the flaws in scientific humanism as a philosophy of life. He closed with a call back to Judeo-Christian foundations and even more to the historic Jesus Christ. Here was answered prayer. Dr. Stamatis had said everything I had longed to say to so many of these friends and colleagues. I was glad that our club members had this opportunity to hear a well-educated man affirm with vigor his faith before a group of people whom they would have considered formidable opponents of the gospel.

8

One to One: Tutoring in the Ghetto

In the summer of 1976 we began moving ahead on plans for a pilot tutorial program for children in the elementary grades. Conrad and I hoped that a framework could be built to stimulate people and churches near or in ghetto areas to use the limited abilities, facilities and finances that most city churches have.

Surely too the churches could help our children develop a greater sense of worth and dignity through these programs. As the children were encouraged and motivated they would improve in their academic skills. As they grew in their understanding of God and of God's plan for their lives, they would desire to please him, and to begin to set higher goals and standards for their lives. We could instill not only the work ethic but the love ethic—an awareness of serving others needier than ourselves.

I was thankful for my previous experience with more formal tutorial programs in the city. I had been especially helped by contact with the Brooklyn College Tutorial Center. I heard they needed someone who could teach English as a second language to parents. So I met the director, Paula Longo, a dedicated teacher of disadvantaged children. In the early sixties Paula had fought to create the Center; she has been able to sustain it through many financial crises ever since then.

Thus in the activist sixties I was exposed to some of the problems and solutions of formal tutoring programs as I observed the Brooklyn College students giving their time and energies. In the seventies, however, the problems were more acute because students no longer could give their time voluntarily. They needed jobs in order to help their parents pay the newly imposed tuition fees at the City University. Paula's problems were made more acute because she could offer only limited hours and a minimum wage.

Yes, tutoring programs done in the official way are expensive and, partially for that reason, ineffectual. If IVCF was going to undertake such a project, it would have to be done with independent financing. Also any sort of moral teaching is virtually forbidden in government-funded programs. Because of cultural pluralism and the fear of misunderstandings and reprisals, teachers are encouraged to abstain from making moral or value judgments. If Inter-Varsity could undertake tutorial projects in local churches with students of various cultural backgrounds, we could teach scriptural truths within the understandable forms of the cultures of the children.

I began gathering materials. Our basic supply came from the public schools in which I had done teacher training as a part of my assignments in the School of Education. I realized that many schools had books which were discarded because they were considered outdated or because they were partially damaged. I also found that local libraries had books which they were willing to lend for this purpose.

At the same time I presented to the executive committee of my own church a written proposal describing how our church could participate in a tutorial program sponsored by IVCF. I chose my own church because of the many children our bus ministry brought from East Harlem. These children were largely Puerto Rican in background; some were Black. The pastor and the church board approved. I was pleased because we could use the church's relatively good educational facilities and because the church would be patient when we made mistakes. No monies, however, were designated, largely because I did not have enough sense to include a budget!

Fortunately, one member of the board, Dr. Stamatis, realized our need. He gave us $500. This helped to pay for carfare for the tutors and for the books and supplies we lacked.

At the same time Conrad and I tried to enlist Inter-Varsity students as tutors. We knew it would not be easy to find them. Most of them needed some kind of summer employment.

Ironically, there was one factor on our side. Unemployment was high among young people so that there were few summer jobs. The Urban Corps in the city was geared more to employ high-school students than college students. The disadvantage was that we had to wait for students to try at least to get a job. I wished we had funds to help them! Only a few days before our training program started enough student tutors had signed up. We had a diverse group to work with, very typical of New York City. Some students were Blacks, some Hispanics (Puerto Ricans and Ecuadorians); one was a Hebrew Christian and a few were Whites.

Several Inter-Varsity staff came from New Jersey each day to help as tutors. Kevin Garcia added good teaching skills and a spicy sense of humor. Cathy, his girl friend, was a special education major who gave technical suggestions. Thom Hopler, an urban ministries specialist for IVCF, gave cross-cultural training to the tutors. Conrad was the coordinator. I was the teaching consultant, giving basic guidelines regarding tutoring. All tutors were required to read Lily Pope's excellent book, *How to Teach Remedial Reading.*

Dave Saez, Dave Cruz and Ketty Santos returned from Nyack College and also offered to help. They were steadily maturing Christians who had come to know the Lord in East Harlem. Helen Weintraub, a Puerto Rican married to a Hebrew Christian, also wanted to help. She too had been part of the Spanish ghetto. Hazel Bateman, our Sunday-school superintendent, tried to help as much as her busy schedule allowed. Hazel and her husband, Sam, could have lived anywhere other than New York City for Sam had a good position as an actuary with Metropolitan Life for many years. They generously poured out their love and their means on the poor and needy of our city.

And then, of course, there was the Chaplain. Daryl, from Massachusetts, was of Portuguese origin. He came to New York on God's call with no connection to any organization. He had been led to our church through a series of providential events. He was a natural leader whose experiences as an army sergeant enabled him to sound commanding and tough but whose heart was yearning with love and compassion. He knew how to organize the children brought to the church. He could keep order and a measure of stability while playing and laughing with them. The Chaplain was inimitable. We all loved him, including Kevin Garcia who often got upset with his antics. He especially hated the Chaplain to call him, "Dear Kevin." And, of course, once the Chaplain knew that, he would give Kevin no peace.

There was another problem. Who was going to drive the bus each day to pick up the children? As I called the available drivers from the church, I realized that we were facing a formidable obstacle. Dennis was taking a summer course. Wes was finishing his dissertation. Charlie worked as an engineer and was not available the hours we needed him. Peter was a third-year student at Cornell Medical School and summer was not a vacation for him. Keith, working on his master's, did not yet have the necessary chauffeur's license he had applied for.

After some agonizing prayer I called Pastor Huamani whose Spanish church was located right in the middle of East Harlem; our children could walk there easily from where they lived. I had not wanted to go to this church because its facilities were inadequate for a tutoring program. There were no rooms large enough to keep the children from distracting one another. I knew that our home church had better facilities. Only later did I realize that this was a blessing.

By having the program at Pastor Huamani's church, we demonstrated that any small ghetto church could have this kind of ministry. Churches in the Spanish ghettos do have inadequate facilities, but high-school and college students of the same cultural background can be the tutors. There are also a few bilingual secretaries and teachers in each church who can coordinate the program. All the necessary ingredients are present. They too can have this ministry.

Yet another problem developed. After the first week a number of our children went to church camp. There was no way to get around it. The only dates our children could attend camp at the reduced rates were early in the summer. We were afraid that we would lose the greater part of the children who had entered the program. However, as we went out to the neighborhood we found that it did not take long to find a completely new batch of children.

This time the Chaplain's disciplinary measures were sorely tested because he was starting with a new group of children who were unused to being controlled. They were also unused to being loved and cared for! The Inter-Varsity staff and students and the church people used all of their ingenuity to find the right balance of love and firmness.

We gradually worked out a reasonable daily schedule. By 9:00 A.M. our tutors were assembled for sharing and prayer. Most of them traveled from one to two hours to be there. By 9:30 most of the children had arrived. We sang a few choruses and prayed; I loved to hear the children pray. The Chaplain had taught them how to talk to God. Then the tutors worked with their children, especially in the areas of reading and math.

After tutoring for about forty-five minutes, we took the children to the church sanctuary for the daily Bible study. The tutors had diverse gifts; we tried to use them all. They took turns telling stories about children in the Bible. Bob did a lot of drawings, comic-strip style, which amused and clarified the stories. Doreen led some lively choruses. The children particularly liked "His Banner over Me Is Love" which she taught with all of the actions. Each day was different and fun. We used large sheets with the words of the choruses and key words from the stories.

Then we had a brief break for refreshments, some fruit juice and cookies. This was followed by another forty-five minute session of tutoring. More educational games were used during this session when it was harder to hold their attention. Some tutors were sitting right next to one another with their children. Wherever the children were, there was chatter and noise. It was not easy, but we knew that they were learning. They kept coming back which meant they liked it too. Some parents cared and sent them early; others did not. If the children did not arrive within a half hour, the tutors would go to their homes to get them. Often neither they nor their parents were out of bed yet!

It was very seldom after the first week that we had the luxury of one child per tutor. By giving each child a well-known achievement test in reading, spelling and arithmetic, we were able to place together children who were on the same level. We also tried to place the children with tutors they felt comfortable and happy with. Children with special learning problems were helped by the more experienced tutors. As teaching consultant I found that my chief role was to help tutors who were in a quandary about how to proceed when their children had particular problems. As I worked with them more and more, I too learned.

Pastor Huamani himself helped with arranging materials and tables as best he could in the space we had. He was excited to see the children learning and our tutors ably relating to them. He had not been sure that non-Hispanics could handle the children. He had secured food for refreshment and lunches from the city summer program. This was a relief because our funds did not stretch! In the afternoon his urban corps workers, high-school students, took the children to a nearby park.

This freed us to tutor junior-high and high-school students in the afternoons. Juan de Jesus, a Puerto Rican, and Anthony Ray, a Black, were junior high-school students who helped to tutor in the mornings. Now they, in turn, could be tutored to improve their skills. We also helped high-school dropouts, like Peter and Willie, prepare to take their high-school equivalency exams. I can still remember the discussions Peter and I had after reading some carefully chosen literature. I fully expect to see the full fruit of God's work in Peter some day.

It was a full schedule but the tutors felt it was worthwhile. Each one could tell a story about "his" or "her" kids. They knew they were ministering not just to minds but to all the needs of these children—spiritual, emotional and physical. How glad I was for the appropriate Christian materials we had added for their use.

I had always hated welfare, but our month of intense involvement in the ghetto made me loathe it intensely. The adults in East Harlem constantly talked about the job they were going to get. Yet they knew they were not going to be employed. The system had them completely enclosed. Once they started working they could be disqualified for welfare checks before they were earning enough to survive. They might have to leave their families in order to be sure basic needs would be met. They realized the problems; for most the risks were too great. And yet their lack of job satisfaction and economic accomplishment was taking them further and further from a sense of purpose and meaning.

God knows we need to work. Indolence in the ghetto leaves people empty and full of a propensity to fill their time with satisfying their own lusts. Parents often are not good parents in part because they do not feel any financial responsibility for their children. If they were responsible, the inability to fulfill these duties would be crushing. Still their surroundings are so depressing that they must long to get out. It takes a lot of hardening to be a second- or third-generation welfare recipient.

It seems that very few people other than those who participate in the churches can ever really break out of the ghettos. An evidence of that is Pastor Huamani's own church. He has watched his congregation turn over many times during the years. His own children live and work in the suburbs. They return to help him from time to time, but they do not want their children to grow up in that environment. I have many Ecuadorian friends who immigrated here about the same time that I returned to the United States in 1968. It is interesting to see that these Christians do not stay in the ghetto. They find jobs and save money until they can move to a better part of the city. I believe this phenomenon occurs because of the moral teachings of the Scriptures.

During the month of the tutoring program, two incidents, instructive of ghetto life, stand out. One morning we had to send a young boy home because he misbehaved beyond toleration. In such cases the Chaplain after fair warning would send the children home to think it over. Usually they returned, having decided to behave. About ten minutes later, this particular boy returned to the church with his adamant mother.

"Who had the nerve to send my son home?"

The reply came back, "Your son would not obey. He was misbehaving. It is very crowded here. We cannot teach when there is disorder. This would bring other problems. He can return tomorrow if he is willing to obey."

The mother stood there for a minute, not knowing how to reply. I stood almost paralyzed waiting to see what this large, heavy-set woman would do. Suddenly she turned to her son who had a stick in his hand. "Bring me that stick!" He stood motionless. "Bring me that stick. I won't hit you. Just bring me the stick." He slowly moved to obey. He knew his mother was embarrassed and angry. He was in trouble. She took the stick and beat him severely in front of the whole group. Then she stalked out of the church basement. The boy, crying, followed her.

The next day I walked down the street to pick up several absentees. She was sitting in front of her apartment building. She often sat there doing nothing on summer afternoons. I greeted her and asked if her son was coming back. "No," she said, "I cannot let him go back."

"But why?" I asked. "Don't you want your son to learn and to do well in school?"

"Yes," she said, "but I can't take a chance of his doing that to me again."

I tried to persuade without success. Her embarrassment and sense of honor outweighed any consideration of her son's academic future. She did not expect him to be able to get out of the ghetto in any case. I left depressed.

I remember another example of the way people think in the ghetto. One afternoon Lydia, a seventh grader, came to be tutored. She was very upset. Her younger brothers and sisters came in the morning.

"I am sorry. I cannot stay today. My little brother, José, has disappeared. My father says he is going to beat me if I do not find him right away. I

know he went with Wilfredo's brother." She pointed to a twelve-year-old boy who had also come for
tutoring. "But I don't know where they went."
There ensued a sharp discussion with Wilfredo
about whether or not he really did know where
José was. I could see that this exchange was not
going to help us in the tutoring or in solving the
problem at hand.

Finally I said, "I'll tell you what. Let's stop for
one minute. We may not know where your little
brother is, but God does. Let's pray and ask God to
bring him back here."

They sat there, rather stunned. I bowed my head
and we prayed. Intensely I told God how important it was to get the tutoring done. We just had to
know where José was. Would he please bring him
back to us immediately? I prayed in Jesus' name.

When I stopped praying an amazing thing happened. Wilfredo stood up and said to Lydia, "All
right. Come with me, and I'll take you to your
brother." I did not say a word as the two of them
left. Would he really do that? Would they come
back? I thought so. About ten minutes later Lydia
and Wilfredo were at the door ready for tutoring!

"My father is not mad anymore. My brother is
home." We went back to tutoring as if nothing had
happened at all. I did thank God for answering my
prayer in the most unexpected way!

Conrad and I were thoroughly relieved when
the tutoring program ended. We were exhausted
from the interaction, from the unexpected needs

we had to fill for materials and counseling and from the constant crossing of cultures. The tutors too were tired from long days, new experiences and surprising events.

I thank God for the results of that weary month. Our church caught a vision of the value of tutoring which it has never lost. Tutoring was made an official part of the church program. We tutor at least one evening each week during the school year. The Chaplain regularly reports improved grades, attitudes and understanding on the part of the children and young people. Spiritual motivation has never been higher.

Our church is not the only one which has profited. Now the students have begun tutorial programs in several other churches. In addition, as a result of sharing what God can do through this means, we have been able to see even more churches take steps in this direction.

9

The Politics of Man

It was fall again, and I was carrying out my normal responsibilities in my division in the School of Education. I was on the usual annual contract with the secondary division and was completing my fifth year. I had been evaluated the previous semester for tenure by the school's appointed committee, and things looked good. I knew that my observation reports from senior colleagues had all been very favorable. I was a doctoral candidate at New York University and had been well recommended by my advisor on the committee. I was active in community projects through my relationship with the Brooklyn College Volunteer Tutoring Program as well as through my teacher and leadership training projects in the Spanish-speaking churches. I was mentioned in the International Scholars Index as well as being a member of the American Association of University Professors. My relationships with my colleagues in the School of Education had been positive as far as I knew. My divisional chairman had given me every indication of her satisfaction with my dedication and my scholarship.

And yet, as I waited for the final response concerning my tenure, a sense of uneasiness set in. Why was it taking so long for this decision to be made? I began to think about the previous year. There is no doubt that I had been fully aware all year of the political ramifications of my sponsorship of the Inter-Varsity chapter. Each time the administration had expressed disapproval, I had realized the possible consequences.

At one point the acting chairman for one semester, Professor Nina Lieberman, had called me to the office. She had received a phone call from Rabbi Fischer. She was tactful in talking with me. I knew she was trying to be fair, and yet . . . would she be? Could she? Later Nina described to me the terrible trauma of being a Jew in Austria when the Nazis came to power. She also told me how she had to begin her studies all over again in England because her previous work was not recognized in the university there. Eventually she had come to the United States where she had gotten her well-earned Ph.D. in developmental psychology at Teacher's College, Columbia University.

Despite these difficulties in her own life, Nina had left me with the impression that she did understand the situation at Brooklyn College. It was possible, she said, that Rabbi Fischer was overreacting. My heart had been eased when she evaluated me while I was teaching one of my larger lecture classes. She had highly approved my teaching and had written a positive evaluation. Surely, I thought, she would be fair in the final countdown! The semester had ended, but the outcome was not to be known until fall.

And now it was fall. I was still waiting. I remember the Friday in November when I had stopped by the divisional office. Professor Svajian was back as our chairman. We had talked about the field-oriented course I was teaching and shared thoughts. Then she paused, looked at me and said, "Barbara, please come to the office on Monday."

Needless to say, I spent a rather difficult weekend. I already knew what she was going to tell me. Yet, no, it could not be so! How could they not grant my tenure? On what grounds? My qualifications were as good, if not better, than others in my division. I asked God to prepare me for whatever the new week was to bring. I remembered the words of the psalmist which had been such a help to me during the difficult year before: "The righteous will never be moved. . . . He is not afraid of evil tidings; his heart is firm, trusting in the LORD. His heart is steady, he will not be afraid" (Ps. 112: 6-8).

On Monday I went to my office after class and prayed for calm and wisdom. I walked down the hall to Room 2606. Yes, Prof. Svajian was waiting for me. I could go in. I numbly sat down. She looked at me and began to weep! My God, what is wrong with this woman, I thought!

"Is your husband well?" She had asked me to pray for him on several occasions because he was ill and was under such pressure because of relatives in war-torn Lebanon.

"Yes, Barbara, he is well—but I have bad news for you. Your tenure has been denied."

I sat there, stunned. So it was true! I had been right in my surmise.

"Why?" I asked. She wept again!

Lord, why is she acting like this? I need to talk to a rational being.

"Barbara, I cannot tell you why."

Lord, how am I supposed to act now? I was still perplexed.

Then I replied, "You don't have to tell me why— I know why. And it is unfair, unjust. You know that!" And then I realized that because she had not been on campus the term before, she did not know all that had occurred. I recounted it to her, sure that she already had other versions of the story. All of a sudden the emotion welled up, and I knew that I wanted to cry my heart out, "Lord, where art thou?" But how could I upset this dear woman any more than she already was? I did not need to tell her that it was unjust. I hastened to leave.

"Barbara," she counseled, "talk to the chairman of the school. In the meantime I will do all that I can . . . but I do not think that we can do much about this now."

"Don't worry," I said, "all things work together for good for those who love God. In the end right has to triumph." They were words, fine sounding words—but did I really believe them?

I walked back down the hall to my office. I had a meeting with Dave TeSelle, my coworker. We had worked together for over a year. I opened the door. Dave saw that I was upset.

"Dave, my tenure has been denied."

"Barbara, oh, you poor gal!"

He jumped up and took me in his arms while I wept like a baby. Then all of a sudden I realized that Dave was another woman's husband. I pulled myself out of his arms, walked to the other end of the office and said, "It's all right, Dave. It's got to be all right. My life is in God's hands. Let's wait and see what happens."

10

Is It Nothing to You?

It has been difficult for me not to moralize in this book. The reader has undoubtedly noticed the times it has slipped through. But I cannot close without a few reflections.

First, we must honor and glorify God for whatever good and whatever progress we made in presenting and living out the truth through the Brooklyn College Inter-Varsity Christian Fellowship chapter. This is the Lord's doing. We are glad of it.

Of course, God was working with human beings who had strengths and weaknesses. I praise him that he takes us seriously where we are, and that he does not obliterate our personalities to do his work. He works in the context of people as individuals.

This is where prayer enters. The story of Inter-Varsity at Brooklyn College would not have happened without the background of prayer. Many ideas, decisions and calculated risks came as I prayed and studied the Scriptures. I prayed much all along—sometimes routinely during my daily devotions, sometimes along the streets of the city, sometimes as a part of a prayer group, sometimes with Pat, my roommate, sometimes with a prayer cell at the college, sometimes with my church at the weekly prayer meeting, sometimes with my faithful friends and supporters at Hephzibah House.

I often prayed alone, crying out to God because fear and inadequacy were overcoming me. I remember one evening when Mary Ann called to tell me about another disruption at the booktable. Some orthodox Jews had become emotional and incited those around to steal our materials. Upset and worried I went to my room and cried to God for his wisdom and protection. I recall that immediately after that prayer the idea of inviting pastors and community people to speak to the dean came to mind. I asked God to confirm the idea. When Conrad concurred, I moved ahead confidently.

Besides my sphere of influence the students also built relationships. Their families, friends and churches prayed. Their pastors came to see our ministry at the annual receptions.

Through prayer has come the direction of God through the Word. I know that on several occasions I acted according to his specific instruction. Several months before I was notified about my tenure denial, God told me in his Word: "For I know the plans I have for you, says the LORD, plans for welfare and not for evil, to give you a future and a hope. Then you will call upon me and come and pray to me, and I will hear you" (Jer. 29:11-12). I had written these verses on a card to memorize and to meditate on. They were of immeasurable help to me during those months of accepting this unexpected change.

I learned throughout the years that the Bible, instead of being a magic formula for bringing about the results you consider desirable, has principles which if adhered to will cause changed situations and lives. I consciously endeavored to bear in mind scriptural injunctions about those in authority as we dealt firmly but courteously with the dean of students. This was true of our dealings with the director of the Student Building. Our relationships with key people have greatly tempered the animosity felt in 1973. Indeed we have found the whole administration more open and helpful.

My attitudes toward minority students in the City University were shaped by the books of the prophets. I read them and studied them. Prophetic concepts began to shape my life so that I could not have acted in any other way without denying strong inner convictions. As difficult as I found it to take a stand, I could remember Jeremiah saying, "If I say, 'I will not mention him, or speak any more in his name,' there is in my heart as it were a burning fire shut up in my bones, and I am weary with holding it in, and I cannot" (Jer. 20:9). Even the context of the prophets seemed to be that of the university at the time when the dean of students was calling me, the student court was trying to uncharter the club and the rabbi had threatened us. I intuitively felt anxious and panicky about my future. "For I hear many whispering. Terror is on every side! 'Denounce him! Let us denounce him!' . . . But the LORD is with me as a dread warrior; therefore my persecutors will stumble, they will not overcome me. . . . Sing to the LORD; praise the LORD! For he has delivered the life of the needy from the hand of evildoers" (Jer. 20:10-11, 13).

The books of the prophets do not only show the dilemma of the prophets themselves. They clearly define the issues, issues very similar to the present reality of the City University. I carefully read Amos and studied Motyer's commentary, *The Day of the Lion.* I looked up every cross-reference. Amos as well as Isaiah was able to pierce through the facade of current prosperity and fantastic economic growth. He saw the terrible oppression of the poor.

Woe to those who lie upon beds of ivory,

and stretch themselves upon their couches,
and eat lambs from the flock,

and calves from the midst of the stall. . . .
Therefore they shall now be the first of those to

go into exile,
and the revelry of those who stretch them-
    selves shall pass away. *(Amos 6:4, 7)*

Woe to those who decree iniquitous decrees. . . .
    and the writers who keep writing oppression,
to turn aside the needy from justice
    and to rob the poor of my people of their right.
(Is. 10:1-2)

Thus says the LORD:
"For three transgressions . . .
    and for four, I will not revoke the punish-
        ment;
because they sell the righteous for silver,
    and the needy for a pair of shoes—
they that trample the head of the
    poor into the dust of the earth,
and turn aside the afflicted."

Woe to those who are at ease in Zion,
    and to those who feel secure. . . .
    (Amos 2:6-7; 6:1)

In New York too the inequities are great. While some live in luxury others are living in densely populated and dirty ghettos. Justice is being turned away. The door for economic betterment was closed at City University when tuition was imposed and when unachievable academic standards were set up. Ghetto schools do not attempt to measure up. Colleges originally built for the poor are the first to be limited and closed. Facilities are allowed to deteriorate. Faculty continue to receive exorbitant salaries, almost the highest in the nation. Areas of the rich and of business are given high priority for police security; low income areas are left to the mercy of the ever growing number of unemployed, embittered young people. Is it any wonder that the students wanted to express concern about these matters, that they wanted to do something about it?

On several pages I comment about sociological models and patterns. I am aware that, according to church growth theory, growth is more likely to occur in homogeneous groups. Our experience both proves and disproves this. Our impossible community was never fully homogeneous. We have always had several ethnic groups represented. Whenever I have thought the group was about to become fully Black or fully White, a new group of freshmen would alter the trend. However, our Black evangelism and our Jewish evangelism show that sometimes it is necessary to give particular emphasis to one group or another to attract their attention and to give them a familiar, comfortable setting.

I might say too that ethnic students have invited me to their churches where I have had an opportunity to minister to their needs in Christian education. At the same time I have endeavored to create confidence in them and their churches about the ministries of Inter-Varsity Christian Fellowship. This was true early in our history because I was already enmeshed in the Spanish community. I spoke in several Black churches, particularly to women's and young people's groups. Later I went regularly to Chinatown where several American-born Chinese congregations had a good number of students in our college.

With God's help we are beginning to get closer to these communities and to minister to them. Many of our students attend churches where other languages are used. The pastors and leaders may not speak English well and are hesitant to become involved at the campus. They need to know how much they mean to us. At the time of crisis for us it was largely White pastors who responded because they knew about Inter-Varsity Christian Fellowship. However, it was clearly the minority pastors concerned for their students who impressed the dean.

We are not an island unto ourselves. We need the whole body of Christ if we are to do God's work effectively and in God's way. The relationship of the club with churches has been enhanced by the insights gained at the annual teas. Many students had been turned off by the institutional churches, but our chapter helped them to return. The student executive committee began to invite pastors to speak at the club on a more regular basis. I know these ministers realized for the first time some of the difficulties the students were having in living out their Christian faith on campus. I am sure that the club was remembered by the churches more often in prayer. Our students attended and got involved. The churches in turn helped us financially in several of the special outreaches the club sponsored. We became part of the community.

My own contribution to the formation of the community was enhanced by the fact that I am an urban person, born and educated in New York City. My later experiences as a missionary for eleven years in South America have been helpful at a time when the city has become multicultural. I have been able to see with more objectivity my own culture; I have been able to relate to other cultures.

But negatively, I have a strong personality. In addition, I had taught for many years in Latin America before I began at Brooklyn College. It was not easy for me to take a more informal, less authority-oriented role. Yet student leadership and initiative were important. It was a temptation to tell the club what to do rather than discuss and share ideas. Waiting for the students to act was not easy for me. But they would grow more if the responsibility for the chapter was theirs.

I remember a painful clash with Russ. I spent a wakeful night, fearful that I had ruined any possibility for further communication. I thank God for Russ's objectivity and humility. He called the next morning. The conversation made me realize that he had seen my intention in spite of my inappropriate reactions. I apologized to him.

I thank God that he uses us in spite of ourselves.

And learning to deal with my own shortcomings was a part of the growth that occurred. God did help me to allow the group to develop its own style and creative approaches. The evidence is the fact that strong student leadership has been developed throughout the years. I could have driven them away.

Any worthwhile service to God, any situation which demands leadership and commitment is going to cost something. I learned to face myself more honestly and squarely when I made mistakes. I also learned to throw off false guilt where an admonition or counsel was misunderstood. I knew when my spirit was right, when I was in control of myself; that it was not wrong to speak as I felt led. God's purpose was to build a community, but the quality of the community was dependent on the quality of the individuals which composed it.

In any adventure of living with God, faith is the necessary ingredient. In order for faith to operate, we must take risks. I call this *calculated* risk for it is based on reason and the direction of the Word of God and the Holy Spirit. As I look back over the past nine years I recognize that God led us from one calculated risk to another and seemed to be asking, "Will you believe that I am with you and that I am guiding you?"

I did not immediately leave Brooklyn College after the tenure denial which is the usual procedure. I was rehired on a semester-by-semester basis as an adjunct lecturer for the next two-and-a-half years by the secondary division of the School of Education. I taught nine hours a week and was able to continue my role as faculty sponsor of the IVCF chapter. The continuation seemed a tacit recognition of my academic competence as well as a grudging recognition of the rights of minority people.

I asked several times about full-time status and tenure, but my chairman seemed to feel this would not be possible. Complicating the problem was the fact that the City University was in serious financial straits. Attrition was being felt. It seemed clear to me that, barring some definite providence of God, I too would not be rehired. I began to consider other options. Perhaps God actually did not want me to be tenured. The university's tenuous future seemed to indicate a redirection of my vocation. This too required faith and vision.

I had felt that God would vindicate me. However, as I have read the Bible, I have realized that God has his own timetable and his own method of righting wrongs. I began to see the disintegration of the City University not only by spiritual forces but also by political and economic pressures. The elimination of open admissions and the imposition of tuition fees tacitly declares that the university is no longer concerned about the poor and disenfranchised of the city, the people for whom it was originally created. The City University of New York has lost its reason to be. It is now self-serving. Demoralization and cynicism pervade its halls.

Cannibalism and distrust are now common among faculty and administration. Students aware of the difficulties are looking for colleges with better facilities, better opportunities and a better spirit.

My experience at Brooklyn College also made me aware of another important concern. Academic freedom is often being severely threatened. The right of expression, a sacred privilege of democracy, gets lip service only. Ironically, it has fallen at the feet of a religion called humanism which was supposed to promote greater tolerance. Humanism has been modern society's replacement for all value systems having universals and absolutes. Man is now the measure of all things; he now determines his own truth. Unfortunately, this religion has a neutralizing effect on morals and values. In order to appear tolerant and broadminded, one must not claim that certain moral standards apply to all. Freedom of expression seems to have become the right to say anything if it will not upset the basic presuppositions of a humanistic majority.

Thus the dean's commitment to toleration and acceptance of the status quo seemed best because administratively no one was supposed to challenge the pluralistic, relativistic views prevalent on the campus. The only way such fragmentation of morals, values and standards can survive is to avoid discussion, interaction and conflict. Students and faculty are taught that it is best to conform—not to question differences. This is stifling and ultimately killing. Surely it should concern the entire academic community. Certainly Christians cannot ignore it. For in such an atmosphere they will necessarily be seen as troublemakers.

If the university is not to be manipulated by expediency and the majority consensus, it must consistently and objectively search for knowledge and truth. Yet it must at the same time exercise tolerance. Love and compassion need to be expressed to the world around the university—a world to which the university should feel responsibility.

New York City, like other large cities, is a bastion of the third world. Believers from the third world now form strong cores in many city churches. They are the fruit of missions abroad. And yet, paradoxically, few people want to minister to them in the city! People have said to me honestly that they would rather serve abroad than work in the inner city. It is indeed a jungle—with an atmosphere of increasing anarchy. Crime is rampant. The welfare ghettos are pitiful sights of debilitated human beings who have never known fulfillment or satisfaction. In the summer of 1977, reportedly 600,000 minority youth were without employment. And without jobs there is no way of acquiring necessary skills or credentials.

And yet, now is a wonderful time for ministering to needy people in urban areas. Many of our IVCF chapters are more alive and exciting than they were throughout the sixties. Our churches are ministering to different areas or communities, reaching out with God's blessing. What is needed are trained and sensitive people in the city helping young people to prepare for leadership and to grow in their understanding of the Word and the church. Our churches desperately need to know how to minister more to the social needs around them too.

I do not know what will happen to our cities. I do not know what will happen to New York. I have a strong feeling, however, that as New York goes, so goes the nation. God has said that he will heal a city if it turns back to him. But one wonders about the concern of the evangelical community for the cities. In Nehemiah's day they did not want to live in the city—and for the same reasons many of us don't want to. It was insecure; there was always the risk of an attack. But Nehemiah reports that "the people blessed all the men who willingly offered to live in Jerusalem" (Neh. 11:2). City churches desperately need to know that the rest of the body of Christ cares.

Jerusalem sinned grievously,
    therefore she became filthy;
all who honored her despise her,
    for they have seen her nakedness;
yea, she herself groans,
    and turns her face away....
All her people groan
    as they search for bread;
they trade their treasures for food

to revive their strength.
"Look, O LORD, and behold,
    for I am despised."
"Is it nothing to you, all you who pass by?"
(Lam. 1:8, 11-12)